Zen and the Art of Resource Editing

The BMUG Guide to ResEdit.

Edited by

Derrick Schneider

Credits

Editor	*Derrick Schneider*
Production Manager	*Hans Hansen*
Assistant Editor	*Noah Potkin*
Publications Coordinator	*Randy Simon*

BMUG would like to thank the following people for their help with this book:

Rett Crocker and *Scott Beamer* for their design ideas
and enthusiasm for the cover.

Tom Chavez for getting us a beta copy of ResEdit 2.1
so that we would be up-to-date when the book was released.

Paul Smallwood, who helped a great deal with the initial steps and
suggesting people who might write for the book.

Casady & Greene, Inc. for their generous donation of
the ChicagoLaser font package.

Editors: *Steve Mills, Dennis Cohen, Steve Webb, Tom DeBoni, Gray Shaw,
Dave Axler, Mike Angell, Steve Costa, Jessica Loveridge, Tim Bodine.*

Dedicated to:

Jeff Songster and *Randy Simon* for their friendship and support.
Randy Futor for placing the idea of this book into my head.

Colophon

This book has been produced using Macintosh computers. The layout was done in Aldus PageMaker 4.0. The typefaces used in the text are ITC Berkeley Oldstyle, ITC Eras, and Casady & Greene's ChicagoLaser. The cover was produced with Adobe Illustrator 3 and Adobe Seperator 3.0; 4-color negatives printed on a Linotronic 300. Draft copies were printed on an Apple LaserWriter IINTX. The final output was on paper to a Linotronic 300 at the facilities of ProPer Publishing, located in Berkeley, California. The book was printed by Griffin Printing & Lithography Co., Inc. in Glendale, California.

Disclaimers and Copyright Information

TABLE OF CONTENTS

INTRODUCTION

It's been more than a year since the idea of doing the BMUG ResEdit book was put into my head. It was at a BMUG meeting, and one of the regulars suggested it, possibly as a casual statement. However, I took it to heart. Sometime during spring semester, I asked our publications coordinator what it would take for BMUG to do a book about ResEdit. The answer was obvious, "A lot of time." When an idea is proposed to BMUG's core group, the person suggesting it is usually smart enough to not take charge of the project. I wasn't. As a result, I became the editor of the book you are now reading.

Since then, the book has gone through a wide variety of ups, downs, and other types of complications. Between lack of articles and budget problems, I am surprised that this book made it through to the printer relatively unscathed. One might wonder if I have learned my lesson about heading BMUG projects. Ask me again when ResEdit 2.2 is on the verge of being released!

When I started this book, I had to tell the people who wrote for it who our audience was. ResEdit is, without a doubt, a tool for programmers who write programs on the Macintosh. It gives one the power to quickly create the resources which are so common among Macintosh applications, and in fact are the roots of the Macintosh interface. However, I am not any kind of a Macintosh programmer, and I used ResEdit all the time. I used it to change my Trashcan, edit my menus, change my watch cursor, and for a variety of other tasks. I knew of lots of people like myself, who used ResEdit to "tweak" their programs in subtle ways. As a result, I decided to aim the book at those people who are like myself. This book is not for progammers. I do not discourage programmers from buying this book, because it still contains a lot of information about certain resources, but this book will not tell you how to create your own TMPLs or about the internal workings of ResEdit itself. For that, I highly recommend Apple's own *ResEdit Reference Manual*. It contains a lot more information which programmers use, and is available from Addison-Wessley.

For those of you who are reading through this book, we have tried to set up, wherever possible, a plan for each article. Within this plan, each section is split up into four areas: the introduction, the editor in question, technical information (where applicable), and a final section talking about tips and additional "exercises" you may wish to try. That way, those of you who already know about what a resource does can skip ahead to the area dealing with the editor itself. Or you may wish to look at the end of the article for new ideas about using this resource.

Some of you may be wondering about the title of this book. It is based on the title of the book *Zen and the Art of Motorcycle Repair*, which has become almost a cliché in the English language. However, it is particularly appropriate for this book. In the minds of most people, the word 'Zen' brings up images of mystical objects and people. The average person would expect a practitioner of Zen philosophy to talk about gateways into other planes of existence, and powerful amulets. In short, Zen represents the mysterious and bizarre. However, the philosophies of Zen, like many other philosophies and religions, try to break very confusing objects and thoughts into individual Truths. To a Zen practitioner, there are certain fundamental Truths which rule the Universe and all things in it.

Both of these definitions of Zen have been incorporated into the title of this book. In the past, ResEdit has always been something of a mystical concept to those who did not know it well. The different plane of existence it represented was a deeper understanding of how a Macintosh worked. As with Zen philosophy, one might hear a variety of ideas about the truths of ResEdit; some of these might be correct, but some would be incorrect as well. This book represents the other view of Zen. In this book, we have tried to break down ResEdit into simple truths which can be applied to many other situations in the computer world. This book, I hope, will give you the confidence to experiment with other resources. Yes, ResEdit can destroy your System and many other things as well. However, if one is careful and follows certain rules, it is possible to become something of a guru of ResEdit itself.

–D.S.

What are resources?

by Brendan McCarthy

Chapter 1

In 1984, when Apple first unveiled the Macintosh, computer users and software developers alike were attracted to the innovative elegance of its now familiar user interface, but the beauty of this computer was more than screen deep. The Toolbox and system software are the Macintosh's fine bone structures, and its brains. They sculpt its features and define its personality. One especially innovative yet hidden aspect of the Macintosh system software which embodies the concept of flexible power is that of the resource. Resources are pervasive and ever-present, and yet most users need never encounter them face-to-face.

So what *are* resources? Simply put, resources are clumps of data. Just about anything can be a resource: the code which applications execute, windows, icons, menus, and pictures are all examples of resources. Every document, application, or system file has a portion which may contain resources, the resource fork. Every resource is uniquely identified by four pieces of information (in order of importance): the file in which it resides, its resource type, its ID number, and an optional name.

Of course, since we are dealing with a computer, after all, this data is really just a stream of incomprehensible numbers. In the early days of Macintosh, creating or changing a resource usually involved a calculator and a large amount of caffeine... Thankfully, some engineers at Apple decided to use their calculators and caffeine-saturated carbonated beverages to make creating and editing resources less of a chore. When they were done a new age dawned, birds sang, flowers bloomed, and ResEdit 1.0 was born. This initial release was a development tool that provided a graphical way to edit many types of resources. However, the original ResEdit was very dangerous, and did very little to help the average user. New versions continued to come out, each with significant improvements. As System 7 became more and more of a reality, Apple realized that they were going to need a new ResEdit which would handle all the new resources in System 7. The most current result of that thought is *ResEdit 2.1.*

The Get Resource Info... dialog box: the beginner's view

When a program needs a resource (for instance, when the *Finder* puts a menu in the menubar), the resource is not created on the spot. This would take a lot of time, and seriously affect the performance of a Macintosh, since the Mac is very resource-oriented. We all know that the Mac moves pretty quickly when it wants to, so the Mac must have another way of storing information—the resource.

What really happens, therefore, is that the program realizes that it needs to put Menu #5 into the menubar. It looks at its resource fork, and pulls out Menu #5. It doesn't look at the menu to see if it says what it should; it just grabs all the info and throws it onto the top of the screen.

What *ResEdit* actually does, then, is allow you to edit resources so that, when the program grabs the resource, it grabs the resource you have put in there.

However, there's a problem with this. As with any Macintosh application, *ResEdit* allows you to copy and paste resources. If you copy another menu resource into the program, the program will never see it, it will just get a little bit fatter. That's because the program is still grabbing Menu #5. This is where the **Get Resource Info...** dialog box comes in.

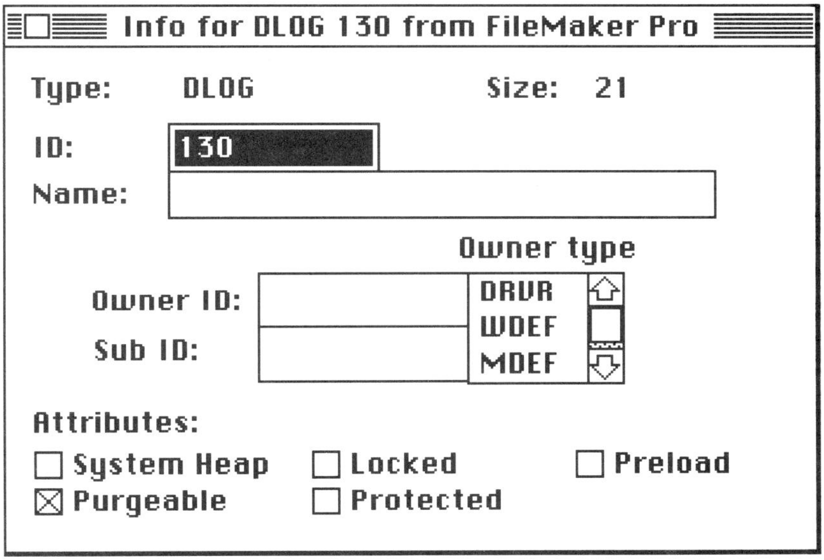

≣☐≣ Info for DLOG 130 from FileMaker Pro ≣≣≣

Type: **DLOG**   **Size:**   **21**

ID: **130**

Name:

Owner type

Owner ID: **DRVR**

Sub ID: **WDEF**

                  MDEF

Attributes:

☐ **System Heap**   ☐ **Locked**   ☐ **Preload**

☒ **Purgeable**   ☐ **Protected**

---

*Figure 1 -
The Get Resource
Info... dialog box.*

This dialog box allows you to change the ID number and name of the resource. Very rarely does a program call a resource by its name, so this field is usually blank. If you wish to change the ID of a resource which you have pasted in or created within a program. Click once on the particular resource (for instance, MENU ID 5 from the *Finder*), and choose **Get Resource Info...** from the **Resource** menu. You will see something very similar to Figure 1. As a beginner, you're only interested in the name and the ID number. If you wish to learn more about the checkboxes below these two fields, see below. However, never change these unless you absolutely have to, and know exactly what you're doing! These boxes, when changed, can cause serious System Errors. If you don't know what you're doing with these, just leave them the way they are.

When changing the ID number of a resource, it is often very comforting to know that *ResEdit* will take good care of you while you're doing this. It will not allow you to change the resource number into something which already exists. You have to first delete or change the ID number of the resource you are replacing, and *then* change the ID number of the new resource. This may seem like a slow way to do things, but a slip of the fingers when typing in a new resource number could be disastrous if *ResEdit* allowed you to directly replace a resource.

Even if you are pasting a new resource into a file, and this resource has the same ID number as a resource which is already there, *ResEdit* will ask you if you want to replace the original resource with the new one, or if you wish to abort the whole operation (the default choice), or if you wish to assign new, unique ID numbers to the new resources. This prevents you from doing anything accidental and ugly!

The Get Resource Info... dialog box for the more advanced user

In additon to the name and ID number of a resource, the **Get Resource Info...** dialog box allows you to change various attributes of the resource, which are represented by the checkboxes at the bottom of the dialog box. As was said before, it is very important that you know what you're doing before you alter these. If a program expects to find a resource, and you have set the "Purgeable" box to true, the program will probably not respond well when it finds out that the resource has been purged out of memory. The only people who really need to know about these boxes are those who are writing their own programs. Some people may have problems with a resource which can be fixed by altering these boxes, but this is a rare case. However, if you are interested in these checkboxes, Figure 3 outlines the function of each one.

Figure 3 -
The meanings of the
checkboxes in the Get
Resource Info...
dialog box

Attribute	If Checked:	If Unchecked:
System Heap	When loaded into memory, the resource is placed in the system heap.	When loaded into memory, the resource is placed in the application heap.
Purgeable	When loaded, the resource may be unloaded if memory gets low.	When loaded, the resource will not be unloaded if memory gets low.
Locked	When loaded, the resource will not move around in memory.	When loaded, the resource may shift in memory to open up free space.
Protected	When unloaded, changes to the resource will not be written back to the resource file.	When unloaded, changes to the resource will be written back to the resource file.
Preload	Automatically load the resource when its resource file is opened (on lunch if it's in an application).	Don't load the resource until it's actually requested.

Zen and the Art of
Resource Editing

As I have said over and over, changing these attributes can cause many problems. However, there are a few common problems which you can avoid. For instance, making a resource available to the System Heap will make it availble to all running applications, but may cause problems if the System Heap is already crowded. If you make a resource purgeable, memory will be freed up if needed, but will no doubt confuse the application looking for a resource which has disappeared. One of the resources which will inevitably cause problems if it has disappeared is the MENU resource. Marking a resource "Locked" may cause memory to fragment (making it harder for applications to get get the amount they request); but an application that assumes a resource will be locked may crash and burn if an unlocked resource unexpectedly shifts in memory. Marking a resource "Preload" may slow down the launch of an application, but the resource will be in memory the instant it's needed. On the other hand, unnecessarily preloading a resource may take up valuable memory.

The best way that I have ever heard the System Heap described is the shaded-in part next to the word "System" in the "About the Finder" dialog box available in the Finder. Similarly, the application heap is the shaded part next to an application in the same dialog box (visible in MultiFinder).

There is one other thing you should know about this dialog box. For instance, there is a restriction on which ID numbers may be used for a resource. Numbers which fall between -32768 and 128 are reserved for the six-colored god, Apple Computer. Everything between 128 and 32767 (including 128) may be used by everyone else.

Playing It Safe

If you keep the following rules in mind, playing with *ResEdit* will be more like a tiptoe through the tulips than a walk through the minefield. They should become mantras to you as you go through this book.

1) Always work on a backup file. Always have a backup of your disk. Never work on the original file. What would you do if you caused a fatal error?

2) Don't change the "Owner ID" and Sub ID" attributes of a resource unless you *really* know what you're doing.

3) Never remove a resource unless you're absolutely sure it's not used. Missing resources can wreak havoc with an application.

4) Never distribute an altered version of an application to anyone else. Users may get confused when things don't look and act like they expect.

As you can see, playing with resource attributes can be like playing with fire, you might burn down the forest, or you might create something fun and interesting.

Manipulating resources with ResEdit.

This section will talk about some of the ways in which resources can be manipulated with *ResEdit*. By the end of this article, you will already be

Chapter 1
What are Resources?

– 9 –

able to do many interesting things with *ResEdit*. The fun starts in the next articles, however, when you'll learn how to actually edit the resources. Here are some concepts which you'll need to know first.

Creating a new resource: When you're in any window of *ResEdit*, except for the editors themselves, you can choose **Create New Resource...** from the **Resource** menu. If you are in the main window of *ResEdit* (the window which shows all the resources in a resource fork), this command will bring up a dialog box which will let you type in the type of resource you wish to create. If you have already opened one of the resource types (by double-clicking on its icon in the main window), and are looking at a list of, for instance, all the MENU resources, this command will create a new resource of that type, assigning it a unique ID number.

Duplicating a resource: One way to make a backup is to duplicate the original resource. Then you can edit the original, and you will still have a safe copy, contained within the file itself. The command for this is **Duplicate** and it is found in the **Edit** menu.

Clipboard actions: As stated earlier, *ResEdit* allows you to copy, cut and paste resources to and from the clipboard. Simply choose a resource (and you can select all the resources of a single type by clicking once on the appropriate icon in the main window) and choose the desired action from the **Edit** menu. With these commands, you can create files of all your favorite resources (such as icons), and copy and paste them when you want to use them.

Selecting multiple resources: Individual resources or resource types may be selected within a group. To select two consecutive resources, hold down the Shift key when you select them. To select non-consecutive resources, use the Command key. If you use the Shift key to select two non-consecutive resources, *ResEdit* will select all the resources between those two resources. This can either be very time-saving or very frustrating if you do it unintentionally.

Practice makes perfect

If you wish to experiment with all these concepts, go right ahead. Make a backup copy of the disk which came with the book, open up *ResEdit* *2.1* (which is on the disk in a self-extracting archive) and play with some of the files on this disk. If you've made a backup (or locked the disk), you won't do any permanent damage, so you can try all of these things.

Happy ResEditing!

Using ResEdit to Customize Your Finder

by Tom Chavez

One of the more fun uses for *ResEdit* is to customize the visual aspects of the *Finder*. Much of what I am covering here can be accomplished with the public domain tool called *Layout* (also sold in the *Norton Utilities for the Mac* package). However, if you were wondering how it all works, here is a good description.

First things first. Launch *ResEdit* and open the *Finder* file. If you are not running under *MultiFinder* (using just *Finder*), you will be able to open the currently running *Finder* file, in your System folder. If you are using *MultiFinder*, you will have to either edit a copy of the *Finder*, or turn off *MultiFinder* and then edit the operating copy.

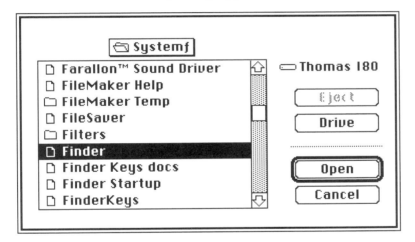

Figure 1 -
Opening the Finder in ResEdit.

The following shows the first window which comes up for the *Finder*. The *Finder* used for the screens shown in this article was version 6.0.7, but the layout information has not changed during the 6.0.x series of *System* software.

The resource type that we are going to be editing is the LAYO resource. This is short for LAYOut, and it controls the way things are set up in the *Finder* windows. Go ahead and open it

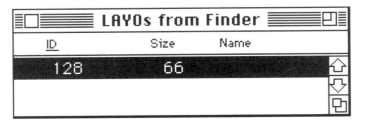

Chapter 2
Customizing Your Finder?

If your copy of the *Finder* is like mine, you should have only one LAYO resource, whose ID is 128. The size is fixed at 66 bytes. Fewer than that would not be enough room for the *Finder* to have all the necessary information. More than that would have extra (useless) information at the end of the record.

One thing you may wish to do is to duplicate the current LAYO ID=128 resource, edit it as a resource with a different ID number, and then switch the two resources so that your changes take affect the next time the Finder is run, such as after a reboot.

For more information about ID numbers and how to change them, see Brendan McCarthy's article "What are resources."

Opening specific resources (such as LAYO ID=128) can be accomplished by double-clicking on the resource, selecting the resource and hitting <Return> or by typing in the name of the resource and hitting <Return>. You only need to type as many letters as needed so that ResEdit knows which one to open. For instance, typing 'L' would select the LAYO resource, since that is the only one which begins with an L.

Customizing

Figure 3 - The LAYO Resuorce.

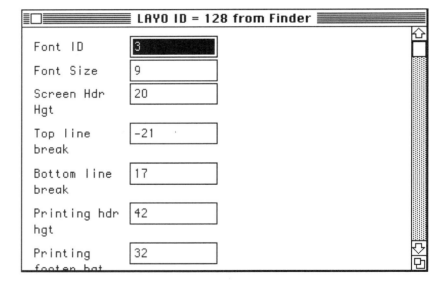

For clarity's sake, I have broken down the four windows of data which make up the LAYO resource into separate fields. I have grouped them roughly by similar function, showing them a few at a time. Therefore, you can skip those fields you already understand, and learn about those which are new to you.

Font ID is the font family number used for displaying text in a window (filenames, dates, etc.). The default is 3 (Geneva). I prefer 33 (Avant Garde). The font size is the size (in points) of the text in all windows, from icon view to small icon view to all of the text views (such as **View by Name** and **View by Date**.)

Confused about fonts and their ID numbers? Read Jens Peter's section about FONTs, FONDs, and other mysterious things.

Screen Hdr Hgt	20
Top line break	-21
Bottom line break	17
Printing hdr hgt	42
Printing footer hgt	32

The Screen Header Height sets how far down in the content area (the actual window, rather than the title bar at the top) of the window the vertical scroll bar and icons start. The default is 20, which allows space for the extra information the *Finder* puts at the top of every window.

The Top line break determines where the first line of text will appear in text views. Don't change this from the default value of -21.

The Bottom line break value determines how much space is left between the last line of text in a text view and the bottom of the window.

The Printing height fields set the header and footer sizes for printed pages.

Window Rect	62	14	250	418	Set

Window Rect is the default size of the window used whenever a new folder is created. Of course the window can be resized after you create it; these values just determine the initial size.

The Set button can be used to make a rectangle without knowing the actual values. When you click on the set button, *ResEdit* expects you to click and drag a rectangle, and that rectangle becomes the Window Rect. One caution: if you click outside of a *ResEdit* window and are running *MultiFinder*, you will be switched out of *ResEdit*, and the rectangle will not be set.

Line spacing	16
Tab stop 1	20
Tab stop 2	144
Tab stop 3	184
Tab stop 4	280
Tab stop 5	376
Tab stop 6	424
Tab stop 7	456
Column Justificatio n	$02

ToolingAround			
Name	Size	Kind	Last Modified
□ INIT-Scope	40K	Control Panel doc...	Wed, Oct 3, 1990 1:32 AM

Line spacing is the point spacing from one line to the next. The default is 16 points. You can increase it for more space between lines in the text views, or decrease it to show more filenames at one time.

The tab stops determine how much space is allotted for the columns which show name, size, kind, etc. Tab stop 1 indicates that the name will start 20 pixels from the left edge of the window. Tab stop 2 is for the size; tab 3 is for kind; tab 4 is Last Modified date; tab 5 is Last modified time; tab 6 is for the lock icon (shown when a file is locked via the Get Info dialog); tab 7 marks the end of the space for the lock icon. The Get Info dialog mentioned here is the one which you can access from the **File** menu in the *Finder*. Do not confuse this with the **Get Resource Info...** dialog box available in *ResEdit*

When a field is justified to the right (rather than the default, left), the text will be closer to the next tab stop, rather than starting from the listed tab. For example, when left justified, the name will start at pixel 20; when right justified, the name will end at pixel 143.

To set the justification, enter a number in the column justification field. Compute this value with the following formula:

Start with 0 (all left justified)

Add 1 ($01) to right justify the Name field

Add 2 ($02) to right justify the Size field

Add 4 ($04) to right justify the Kind field

Add 8 ($08) to right justify the Last Modified date field

Add 16 ($10) to right justify the Last Modified time field

Add 32 ($20) to right justify the lock field.

As shown above, the justification is set to right justify the size field. This makes the sizes line up in a nice column with the "K"s all in a line, rather than lining up the first digits in a column.

A quick lesson about hexadecimal vs. decimal. In *ResEdit*, a "$" preceding a number indicates that it is in hexadecimal, or base–16. Base–16 counts a bit differently than regular decimal:

0 = $0	8 = $8	16 = $10	24 = $18
1 = $1	9 = $9	17 = $11	25 = $19
2 = $2	10 = $A	18 = $12	26 = $1A
3 = $3	11 = $B	19 = $13	27 = $1B
4 = $4	12 = $C	20 = $14	28 = $1C
5 = $5	13 = $D	21 = $15	29 = $1D
6 = $6	14 = $E	22 = $16	30 = $1E
7 = $7	15 = $F	23 = $17	31 = $1F

As you can see, hexadecimal doesn't become two digits (carry over) until sixteen is reached, at which point it carries a one to the next higher digit, just like base–10. At the next multiple of sixteen, it carries over again to become $20.

If this doesn't make much sense to you, that's probably because you were born with ten fingers rather than sixteen. *ResEdit* will let you use decimal values instead of hexadecimal. Just enter the appropriate decimal value, and make sure that you do not include the dollar sign.

Reserved $00

Bad karma can come from editing reserved fields. Not only that, but it can cause serious problems with your desktop!

The next three fields all control the layout of icons in the view by icon mode.

Icon Horizontal spacing sets the amount of pixels between icons next

Icon Horiz. spacing   48

Sm. Icon Horiz.   96

Icon Vert. spacing   45

Sm. Icon Vert.   20

Icon Vert. phase   0

to one another. The default for this is 64; as you can see, I space my icons a bit closer together.

The Icon Vertical spacing sets the pixel spacing between the icons vertically. The default for this is also 64, but 45 is enough so that the second row of icons appears just below the text (names) for the first row.

Phase determines whether all of the icons appear in a straight row, or if they are staggered up and down, with every other icon at a different vertical offset from the previous one. This can be useful for long filenames that tend to run into each other. Just set the vertical phase to something like 32, and the names will not run into each other.

The two fields which control Small icons are exactly like the fields which control large icons. The Small Icon Horizontal controls the horizontal spacing of icons in the small icon view. The Small Icon Vertical controls the vertical spacing.

Default view   1

The Default view is the window type that will be used when new windows are created. The choices are:

0	small icon view
1	icon view
2	by name
3	by date
4	by size
5	by kind

Text view date $\boxed{\$0200}$

The Text view date field controls how the date is shown in any of the text views. There are three formats for the date field:

$0000	short date	e.g. 10/3/90
$0100	long date	e.g. Wednesday, October 3, 1990
$0200	abbreviated	e.g. Wed, Oct 3, 1990

The following are a set of True/False (or just Yes/No) choices that you can make for certain built-in features of the *Finder*. In these choices, 0 equals false (or No) , 1 equals true (or Yes).

Use zoom Rects	⦿ 0	○ 1
Skip trash warnings	○ 0	⦿ 1
Always grid drags	○ 0	⦿ 1
Unused 4	⦿ 0	○ 1
Unused 3	⦿ 0	○ 1
Unused 2	⦿ 0	○ 1
Unused 1	⦿ 0	○ 1
Unused 0	⦿ 0	○ 1

Use Zoom Rects will control whether or not the fancy animated zooming rectangles will be used whenever you open or close a folder or disk. I turn these off just because they take time to happen, and I want my windows opened and closed more quickly.

The Skip Trash Warnings choice lets you get rid of the safety dialogs "Are you sure you want to throw away the application <name>?" and "Are you sure you want to throw away the system file <name>?". You can also prevent this from happening by holding down the option key when you throw away a file. This button allows you to set the default. If you are prone to throw away things that you don't mean to, set this to false (click the '0' radio button).

Always Grid Drags turns on the icon locking that prevents a window from having icons all cluttered over each other. This forces an icon onto the grid set by the horizontal and vertical spacing. Setting this to true helps you stay neater. In fact, you won't be able to put an icon off of the grid.

The Icon-Text Gap increases the distance between an icon and the text which falls below it. If you want to put some space between your icons and their names, set this to a higher value.

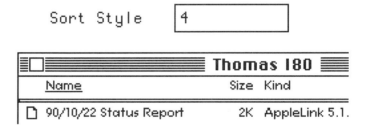

At the top of the text view windows, the field which was sorted (e.g., date when viewing by date) is underlined. In the illustration, a "view by name" window, the word "Name" is underlined showing that the sort took place with that field.

If you would like a different style used for the text of the "view by" field, such as bold italic, enter a number based on this formula:

Start with 0 ($0)

Add 1 ($1) for bold

Add 2 ($2) for *italic*

Add 4 ($4) for underline

Add 8 ($8) for outline

Add 16 ($10) for shadow

Add 32 ($20) for compressed

Add 64 ($40) for expanded

So for *bold italic*, the magic number would be 3 (1 for bold + 2 for italic).

The Watch Threshold controls how quickly the cursor will switch to a watch for time consuming operations. The number is measured in ticks, which are 60-ths of a second. As shown, the watch cursor will not be shown until two seconds after a process starts. For tasks which take less than two seconds, you won't see the watch. For longer tasks, it will come up after two seconds.

Unused 7	⦿ 0	○ 1
Unused 6	⦿ 0	○ 1
Unused 5	⦿ 0	○ 1
Unused 4	⦿ 0	○ 1
Use Phys Icon	⦿ 0	○ 1
Title Click	○ 0	⦿ 1
Copy Inherit	○ 0	⦿ 1
New Fold Inherit	○ 0	⦿ 1

HyperCard Help

HyperCard Program

Audio CD 1

Use Physical Icon replaces the standard disk, CD, and hard drive icons with pictures representing their physical locations. There are icons for the Mac Plus, SE, II, IIcx, Portable, etc. These icons help you see exactly which disk you are using.

Title Click lets you double-click in the Title bar of a window to open up its parent window. For example, if you are looking at the system folder on your hard disk, and your hard disk window is not showing, with this set, you can double-click on the title bar, and the hard disk window would open and come to the front. This is a good way to wind back out from a deep folder if you've cleaned up the parent windows.

Copy Inherit sets whether a copy of a folder inherits the original's colors, view by setting, etc.

New Folder Inherit determines whether a new folder will have the same color, view by setting, etc. of the parent folder.

Color Style determines how icons are filled in on color systems:

0 means that the black pixels are colored

1 means that the white pixels (interiors) are colored

```
Max # of        ┌──────────────┐
                │ 20           │
windows         └──────────────┘
```

For those with lots of screen real estate, the standard 13 open window maximum may not be enough. I have raised my maximum to 20 and find that if I open more windows than that, I cover up too much space on the screen.

You may need to raise the *Finder's* memory partition size (using the Get Info box in the *Finder*, after selecting the *Finder* itself) to something larger. If you do a lot of file copying, especially of large files, and have allowed many windows to be open you may need to increase it as well. In my 8 Meg system, I raise it to 400K.

```
╔═════════════════════════ Info ═════════════════════════╗
║ ▫                                                       ║
║                                          Locked  □      ║
║     ┌─────┐                                             ║
║     │▭▭▭▭ │   Finder                                    ║
║     │     │   System Software Version 6.0.5             ║
║     └─────┘                                             ║
║       Kind: System document                             ║
║       Size: 109,185 bytes used, 108K on disk            ║
║                                                         ║
║                                                         ║
║      Where: Thomas X80-2, SCSI 6                        ║
║                                                         ║
║                                                         ║
║    Created: Wed, Mar 7, 1990, 12:00 PM                  ║
║   Modified: Fri, Nov 2, 1990, 9:34 PM                   ║
║    Version: 6.1.5, © Apple Computer, Inc.               ║
║             1983-90                                      ║
║    ┌────────────────────────────────────────────────┐  ║
║    │                                                 │  ║
║    │                                                 │  ║
║    │                                                 │  ║
║    │                                                 │  ║
║    └────────────────────────────────────────────────┘  ║
║      Suggested Memory Size (K):   160                   ║
║                                       ┌──────┐          ║
║    Application Memory Size (K):       │ 400│ │          ║
║                                       └──────┘          ║
╚═════════════════════════════════════════════════════════╝
```

Well, we've reached the end of the LAYO resource. With the tips above, you can change the look of the Finder to suit your own needs. You might want to write down what you change, as it will not be maintained when you install the next version of system software. Many times I've forgotten what I've changed, so I edit some parts, and then exit *ResEdit*, only to see that it just doesn't look the same. So now I have a list next to my Mac.

Now you might have some time to further customize your Finder by changing cursors (in CURS), dialog and alert layout (in DLOG, ALRT, and DITL), icons (in ICN#), menu text and command keys (in MENU), or small icons (in SICN). These are all covered in other sections of this book.

Have fun. And remember, *always work on a copy of your source file.* You'd hate to lose your only copy! And when you have something you like, make a backup copy.

Tom Chavez is the ResEdit *Product Manager for Apple Computer, Inc. He was a co-founder of BMUG back when it was run by Tom, Raines, Reese, and a core team. Tom has worked at Apple for the past two and a half years since he graduated from U.C. Berkeley. Tom can be reached on AppleLink at Tom.Chavez or on the InterNet at tomc@apple.com.*

Chapter 2
*Customizing Your
Finder?*

I Think ICON.

by Derrick Schneider

Chapter 3

Everyone in the Macintosh community knows what icons are, even if they don't know what they're called. Every time you start up your computer or quit an application, you see the icon of the Trashcan. Whenever you put in a floppy, you see the disk icon. If you have a hard drive (and it's healthy) you see its icon. But icons can exist in other places as well. Dialog boxes frequently have icons in them (see Figure 1). Sometimes menus have icons next to the items in the menu. Icons are, in short, one of the integral parts of the Macintosh interface.

Figure 1 - Common Icons

These icons, after a little while, can get boring. Sure the trashcan icon gets the point across, but don't you wish you could make it look like a toilet? With *ResEdit*, you can do just that.

During the course of this article, 'icon' will refer to both ICN#s and ICONs. The specific terms will be used if referring to one type or another.

Though all icons look alike to the user, there are actually two different types of black & white icons: ICN# and ICON . These terms are the names of the resources which contain these icons. Okay, so what's the difference? The basic difference is where the icons are used. ICN#s are used by the *Finder* and the *Desktop* files or by applications when a special object named a mask is needed (see below). ICONs are used within a program. For example, let's take a look at *HyperCard*. If you use *ResEdit* to open *Hyper-Card*, you will see both ICN# and ICON resources (see Figure 2). Open the ICN# resource (Just look for now). You will see the two icons which you see in the *Finder*: *HyperCard* itself and the icon for a stack. Now close this, and open the ICON resource. You will see all of the icons which you have probably seen when choosing an icon for a button.

Figure 2 - The two different types of icons in HyperCard 2.0

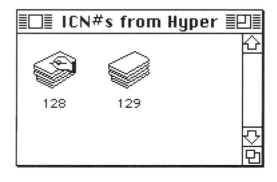

Zen and the Art of Resource Editing

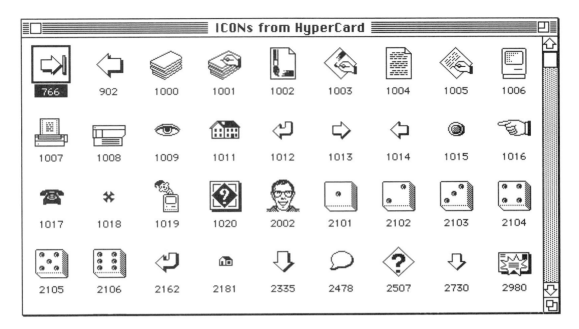

766	902	1000	1001	1002	1003	1004	1005	1006
1007	1008	1009	1011	1012	1013	1014	1015	1016
1017	1018	1019	1020	2002	2101	2102	2103	2104
2105	2106	2162	2181	2335	2478	2507	2730	2980

EDITING ICONS

Now you know what the two types of icons are: so what? You probably want to go ahead and do something really cool to them, right? Okay, let's edit some icons. Make a copy of *HyperCard* if you learn only one thing from this book, let it be that you should always work on a backup copy of a program when using ResEdit unless you're really sure of what you're doing!. Open your copy with *ResEdit*, and open the ICON resource (we'll get to the ICN# resource in a bit). You can either edit an existing ICON, or choose Create New Resource from the Resource menu. In either case, you will get a window very much like that shown in Figure 3.

Now what? The icon editor features a simple selection of tools you can use to edit an icon. These are tools which are familiar from many of the available painting and drawing programs. There is also a pattern palette which can be accessed by holding down the mouse button while clicking on the black rectangle below the tools. After a short time, the palette will appear. If you then move the mouse beyond its boundaries, it will "tear off". You then have a pattern palette you can put anywhere on your screen. Note that the "black rectangle" actually fills with whatever pattern you have selected currently. Be sure to save your changes, and that's all there is to it!

ICN#s are a little bit different. To see why, open a copy of the *Finder* with *ResEdit*, and then open the ICN# resource. Open the empty trashcan icon. This editor is bigger and has more views of the icon in a variety of situations. This is because ICN#s have some important differences from ICONs

For a more complete description of the available tools, see the "Quick Review of Paint Tools" section

Chapter 3
I Think ICON.

Figure 3 -
The ICON editor

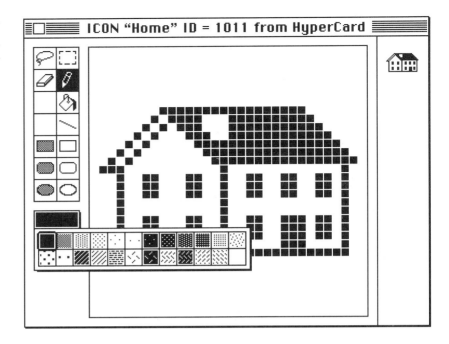

If you've edited the icon for an application, you'll need to rebuild your *Desktop* (hold down Command and Option when booting or inserting a disk) in order to see it. When the *Finder* needs an icon to represent an application, it stores it in the *Desktop* file so it doesn't take as much time to retrieve it. Even after editing your icon, the *Finder* will still look for the icon in the old *Desktop* file. By rebuilding your *Desktop*, you force the *Finder* to store your new icon in a new *Desktop* file. An important note: If you have any comments in the "Get Info" dialog boxes in the *Finder*, they will be erased when rebuilding the *Desktop*.

THE MASK

So what's different about these two icons? What do ICN#s need that ICONs don't? I'll answer this with a question: What happens if you click once on an icon in the *Finder*? The icon usually becomes an inverse of itself, so that you know which icon you have selected. What happens to the folder icon if you open it? It becomes filled with a pattern, right? These things are all controlled by an ICN#'s mask, as it's called. This is the difference between the two types of icons.

In the good old days of the Macintosh, this mask could be edited so that when you clicked once on an icon in the *Finder*, it would look different. These were called "animated icons". For instance, some people might edit the mask of the folder icon so that if you selected it, it would look like an open folder. This is still possible in theory, but Apple no longer supports animated icons. The mask, in essence, controls how the icon looks when selected. Some icons, when selected, look and act considerably different.

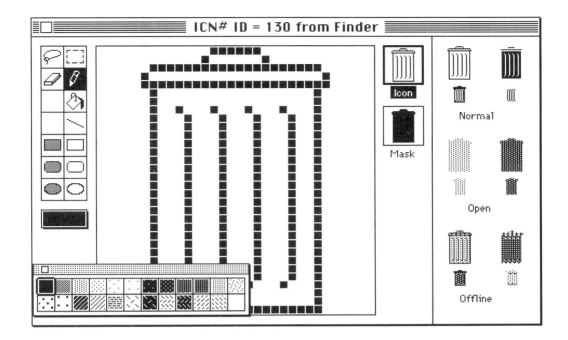

Icon

Mask

Normal

Open

Offline

The best example of this is *HD Backup*, which Apple provides with its system software. When you select this icon, it appears as if the two halves are not connected. This is because of the mask. If you click between these halves, you'll notice that you can't move it. It's as if you're not clicking the icon at all. This, too, is because of the mask.

To create a mask drag the image of the ICN#, directly to the right of the editing area onto the panel which is labeled with the word "Mask." ResEdit will automatically create the necessary mask. If you do wish to experiment with how the mask works, you can bring up its editor by clicking once on the "Mask" panel.

At the right edge of the ICN# editor, you get to see how your icons look in a variety of situations. With these images, you can determine how your mask looks and behaves. The first row, "Normal", shows your icon and its mask behaving normally. The little tiny icons below it (SICNs) are used when viewing by small icon. Below that, you see a row labeled "Open". This is what the icons will look like when you have that application open under *MultiFinder*. The third row, "Offline", shows what the icons will look like if the disk they are on has been ejected.

EDITING AROUND THE OFFICE:
ICONS YOU MAY WANT TO EDIT

One of the most common icons which people edit is the Trashcan icon. Mine has gone through a whole range of shapes: dumpster, shark, black hole, monsters, and Oscar the Grouch. To edit this, open the *Finder's*

FIGURE 4 -
The ICN# editor

Chapter 3
I Think ICON.

– 25 –

ICN#s (Remember to practice on a copy!). You will notice that there are actually two trashcan icons; one used when the trashcan is "empty" and the other used when the trashcan is "full".

While you've got this window open, you'll see that all the icons you're used to seeing in the *Finder* can be edited here. However, one of these is a lie. Many people want to edit the way a disk will look when it is inserted in the drive, so they edit the floppy disk they see in the *Finder*. However, this is to no avail. The icon for an inserted floppy disk is built into the ROMs of your Macintosh. This disk is actually used very seldomly. Well, it was worth the shot, anyway.

Often, a person who feels comfortable editing icons will go in search of the hard disk icon, so that he or she can change that. Again, to no avail. This is usually not easily done. The hard drive icon is frequently stored in the hardware of the drive itself. Sometimes, you can find the icon in the formatter for the drive, but that is rare, and it is not reccommended that you change it even if it is there. For changing your hard disk icon, I recommend an INIT known as *Façade*. This little program, by Greg Marriott, allows you to associate names of icons with names of disks. To change your hard disk icon, open the file *FaçadeIcons*. You then find an icon you like (an ICN#), and change the name of the icon so that it matches the name of your hard drive (or any other disk). This is done through the **Get Resource Info...** dialog box within *ResEdit*. Make sure *Façade* and *FaçadeIcons* are in your System Folder, and restart your computer.

If you wish to add icons to *HyperCard*, you can add them by opening the resource fork of the stack you wish to put them in. If it is a new stack, *ResEdit* will probably tell you that the stack has no resource fork, and you're about to create one. Don't worry about this. It just means that no extra resources have been added yet. Keep in mind that if you're going to distribute a stack with an extra icon (one not supplied by *HyperCard*), the icon needs to be placed in the resource fork of the stack itself. That way, the icon will always be available. Remember that icons used within stacks are ICONs, and not ICN#s.

Color icons

by Lisa Lee

Color icons have been around since Apple first unveiled the Macintosh II. The new possibilites of color introduced many new resources to deal with the world beyond black-and-white. Among these new resources was the cicn, short for Color ICoN. However, it was not used very effectively. Editing them required programs other than *ResEdit*, and placing them on the desktop required still more programs, outside of the system software.

With System 7.0 approaching quickly, Apple has created two new types of color icon resources, the icl and the ics. The two are very closely related (icl is the large icon, and ics is the small icon used by *MultiFinder*) and each one is split into two parts. icls are split into icl8 and icl4, which are for 8-bit (256 colors) or 4-bit (16 colors) respectively. Similarly, ics resources are either ics8 or ics4. In the System 6.0.x series, these new icons are not seen by the system (see below for installing them onto your desktop under System 6). However, System 7 will theoretically recognize these resources without the use of any additional programs.

Icons are now divided into families, which means that you no longer have to create separate resources; they are created automatically.

The icl and ics editors

To see what an icl looks like, set your computer to either 256 colors or 16 colors, depending on how many you have available. Use *ResEdit* to open the *System* file. System 6 does not have the icl8 resource already installed. In order to see what one looks like, use the **Create New Resource...** command from the **Resource** menu. You will then see a dialog box like the one shown in Figure 1. In the field, type the word icl8 (if you're set to 256 colors) or icl4 (if you're set to 16 colors). Press <Return> and you will see the editor shown in Figure 2.

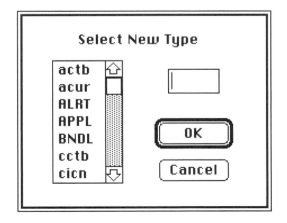

Chapter 4

*Figure 1 -
The Create New
Resource... dialog box*

Figure 2 -
The icl editor

Using the icl editor

For more information about using the paint tools, see "A Quick Review of the Paint Tools."

The most prominent feature of this window is the FatBits window showing a blown up version of the color icon. Along the left of the window is the area filled with all the familiar paint tools. There is one new tool, the color dropper, which is described below. Below this, you will see the selection of colors (as a pop-up, tear-off palette), which will vary depending on how many colors you have. You will also see the pattern palette, which is very similar to the one in black-and-white editors (the only difference being the additon of a few colors). Directly to the right of the editing area, you can see the actual-size icons for icl8s, ics8s, icl4s, iclss, and ICN#s (ics#s are the new version of small icons for ICN#s), as well as the mask which is responsible for each of them. If you click on each of these, the individual editor for that icon will be brought forward. This provides a quick way to toggle between the different types of icons used in the *Finder*.

More information about masks is presented in the section about ICONs and ICN#s.

To the far right, you can get an idea of how your icons will look when in a variety of situations. In each of these sections, the normal icon is on the right side and the selected icon is on the left side. "Closed" shows you what the icon looks like when sitting patiently on the desktop. "Open" shows you the icon when it is open under *MultiFinder* or (in the case of the *Finder*) opened on the desktop (such as folders and hard drive icons). "Offline" shows you what the icons looks like if they are visible when the disk it is on is ejected. Note that each of these will only show what the current icon will look like. If you are editing an icl8, and wish to see how the icl4 looks, simply click on the icl4 icon to the right of the editing area, and *ResEdit* will re-adjust the views.

Zen and the Art of Resource Editing

Those are the basics of the icl resources. ics resources are exactly the same, except for the fact that the editing area is a little bit smaller (a 16 X 16 grid as opposed to the full 32 X 32 grid for an icon). The paint tools for color editors are a little bit different than for black-and-white icons, and those will be described now.

The new color tools

The most radical difference between the color paint tools and the black-and-white tools is the color dropper, shown as a small eye dropper. This tool can be very useful, especially when using 256 colors. If you click with the color dropper on a pixel, the color will be set to the color of the pixel you have clicked on. Thus, if you are creating an icon and you wish the upper right to be the same color as the lower left, but can't quite tell which shade of grey you used in the lower left, simply click in the lower left with the color dropper. Then you can color in the upper right area.

This leads to the next new tool, the pencil. In a black and white editor, using the pencil to click on a pixel does one of two things: turns it off or turns it on. In a color editor, this is a little bit different. If you click on a pixel which is a different color than the selected color, the pixel you have clicked will become that color. If, however, you click on a pixel which is the same color as the currently selected color, that pixel will become white.

All the paint tools except the eraser use the selected color. The eraser will make everything white.

Installing your new icons: pre-System 7

To use your color icons on the desktop, you should use a program called *Sundesk*, by Tom Poston (included on this disk). To use it, do the following:

First, open up the file *SunDesk Icons*. Second, use *ResEdit* to open the *DeskTop* file (you cannot be under *MultiFinder* when you do this). Click once on the ICN# icon in the *DeskTop* file, and choose **Copy** from the **Edit** menu. Then go to the *SunDesk Icons* window, and choose **Paste** from the **Edit** menu. That will provide you with the icons from your desktop.

Open up the ICN# you wish to colorize, and choose the icl8 or icl4 editor (click on the appropriate icon directly to the right of the editing area). Then use the tools described above to color this icon. Important: Do not change the shape of the icon itself! You can color its edges and insides, but do not color beyond the edges of the icon itself. If you do, the icon will not look good, because the mask will not have have been altered to accomodate the new shape.

Save your changes, make sure the files are where they are supposed to be (i.e., the System Folder), and restart your Macintosh. You will then see your new color icons!

Some tips on creating color icons

1)   Try to sketch out what the icon will look like on regular paper before sitting down in front of your Macintosh. Try not to create the icon pixel-by-pixel. Instead, try to draw as if your mouse were a normal writing instrument like a pen or pencil. I find it easier to create the original icon in black and white and, as I add color, modify the icon until it looks usable.

2)   Experiment with different colors. Don't feel a need to stick to colors that are physically located near to another color. Try to visually match the shade of a normal color (or try to imagine the color you would like to use in your mind) and find the matching color on the pallette.

3)   Once you have a rough outline of the icon, you can move the whole rough image or parts of it with the marquee tool. If the outline tool is double clicked, the whole image is selected in the icon creation window and you can position it anywhere within the icon window.

4)   When you are finished with the icon, be sure to choose **Remove Unused Colors** from the **Color** menu. When *ResEdit* first creates the icon, it includes all the colors into the size of the icon, taking up unnecessary memory. This menu command will remove all the colors you did not use when making the icon.

5)   Always make sure, if you have an 8-bit computer, to make 4-bit icons as well. That way, your desktop will still be in color even if you switch to 16 colors. Also, if you give your artwork to a friend who uses 16 colors, the icon will just look like the black-and-white icon for the file.

6)   If you do use someone else's icls, be sure to use the **Get Resource Info...** dialog box to make sure the ID numbers match. When you create an original piece of art, *ResEdit* will make sure that all the members of the icon family will have the same resource number. However, other systems may have different IDs, in which case *SunDesk* will not recognize them as being associated with your black-and-white icons.

Replacing the Watch Cursor

by Rick Reynolds

There are two kinds of resources which determine the appearance of your cursor on the screen: CURS and acur.

These two resources are used at different occasions. The CURS resource determines the physical appearance of a cursor. The acur is used to animate a cursor when your Macintosh is busy executing commands that do not show much activity on the screen. You then get some signal that your Macintosh is working on something and cannot speak to you.

Both of these resources are designed to be modular in nature, and you can change them much like changing the compact disc in your CD player or the clothes on your Barbie Doll.

ResEdit allows you to alter these resources to produce interesting effects. With it, you can design your own watch cursor, and replace the one which comes with the *Finder*. If you're not artistically inclined, you don't need to design these resources yourself. You can download them from networks, borrow them from other applications, or get them from your friends. Then all you have to do is quickly insert them into the resource fork of the application.

Getting our hands dirty

Let's take a look at these resources. Use *ResEdit* to open a copy of the Finder. Open up the CURS resource in the *Finder* by double-clicking on it.

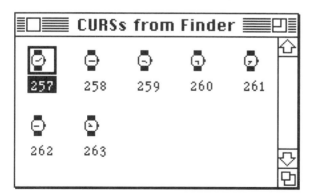

The items in the window are the various CURS resources and their numerical designations. Each CURS can have its own name, but the Macintosh operating system tracks these resources by number, not name. Clicking once on any of these small CURS resources will select it. With the CURS resource selected, you can copy or cut the resource onto the Clipboard, for later use within *ResEdit*. You can also access the **Get Resource Info...** menu command to change the cursor's ID number and name. To get to the CURS editor, double-click on a single CURS resource. Open CURS ID #257 in the copy of the Finder which you have opened.

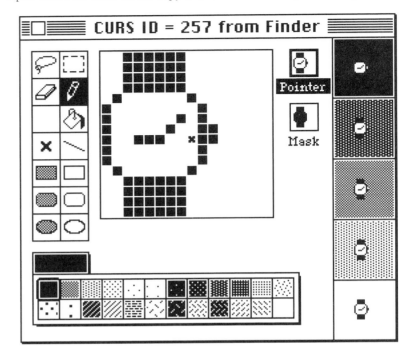

This FatBits editor will look very different for those who have used previous versions of ResEdit. It features several new features, and can be used to quickly make complex cursors. The biggest part of the editor is the editing area, which shows the selected cursor, but enlarged for easy editing. To the left of this is the area where you choose a painting tool. *For more information about paint tools, see "A Quick Review of the Paint Tools."* Directly below this is the pattern palette, which can be pulled off and moved to a convenient place. To see it, hold the mouse button down over the rectangle below the paint tools. Directly to the right of the editing area are two small windows "Pointer" and "Mask." With these small windows, you can quickly move between the cursor and mask editors. For more information about cursor masks, see below. At the far right of the window, ResEdit shows you your cursor on a variety of different patterns.

The Hot Spot Of A Cursor

All cursors have a single pixel which is considered "the hot spot." The hot spot is the active part of the cursor. Think about the arrow cursor for a minute. When you click on an object (such as a close box or an icon) with the tip of the pointer, something usually happens. What would happen if you clicked on something with the base of the arrow (the thin part)? Nothing would happen. This is because the hot spot of the arrow is at the very tip. Therefore, no matter how big your cursor is, the Macintosh is only concerned with a single pixel, the hot spot.

To create a new hot spot within a cursor, choose the hot spot tool (it looks like an X). Then, click in the editing area to place it. That's all there is to it!

There are some design tips which you should follow, however. When placing a hot spot, it's important that the user can easily know where it is, even if they don't know what a hot spot is. Some examples of good places are at the end of a pointed area (as in the arrow), in the middle of crosshairs, or in the center of a symmetric shape (the center of a circle, for instance).

Another design tip is useful for animated cursors such as the watch. With these, you should make the location of the hot spot consistent. In the watch, it would be very confusing if the hot spot were placed at the end of the moving hand in each frame. Instead, you could put it on the "dial" of the watch (or slightly to the left, as Apple did). The important thing is that you don't keep changing the conditions for the user.

The Mask

Cursor resources, like ICN#s, have an attribute known as a mask. In ICN#s, the mask controls how the icon looks when selected or open, as well as how the icon looks against various backgrounds. In cursors, the mask is only responsible for how the cursor looks when seen on a background. Creating a mask is very simple. Drag the image from the "Pointer" area into the "Mask" area, and *ResEdit* will create the appropriate mask.

Sometimes, however, this mask may not be perfect. For instance, look again at Figure 3. Look at the cursor on the black background, and you will see that the only visible part of the cursor is the face. To fix this, simply edit the mask. Click once on the "Mask" window to bring up the mask editor. Now surround the cursor with a line which is one pixel thick. Your watch is now completely visible on a black background. Incidentally, this is what happens when you place the black arrow cursor on a black background. The mask keeps it visible.

As you are designing, it often helps to try out your cursor. **Try Cursor**, from the **CURS** menu, allows you to work with the new CURS resource. This menu selection is actually a toggle switch so you use the new cursor until it is turned off. When you wish to look at the arrow again, simply choose this menu option again. Note: under *MultiFinder*, you will only have the new cursor within *ResEdit*. If you switch applications, your cursor switches to the resource fork of the active application. Your cursor will also revert if you go to another window in *ResEdit*.

With the concepts above, you can easily add single cursors (non-animated) to any application. You can also edit existing cursors if you wish. Adding new cursors won't usually do anything, since the program doesn't expect to find new stuff there. However, *HyperCard* will let you show an original cursor from a script. Refer to your instruction manuals for more information on how to do this.

acurs: Animating Your Cursors

When you do something which is very time-consuming on your Macintosh, you usually see some sort of animated cursor, telling you that the Macintosh is still active but busy. This animation sequence is controlled by the acur resource (Animated CURsor). To get an idea of how this works, open the acur resource in a copy of the Finder.

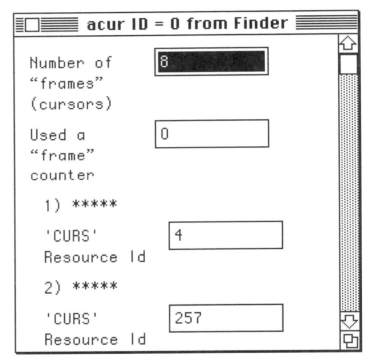

Figure 6 -
The acur editor

The acur editor provides you with a lot of areas to look at. The values in this window can be changed as if you were in a word processor. The first field, Number of "frames" (cursors) is the field which determines how many frames are in the animated cursor. In the watch cursor, there are 8 frames.

The second field can be filled with a number which will determine the number of ticks (60ths of a second) between frames of the animated cursor. If you wish to slow your cursor down for visual effect, change this number. Normally, it is left at 0, with no time between frames. You will need to play with this number to determine the appropriate number for your particular cursor.

The rest of the fields describe the order in which the frames are shown. That way, the sequence is correct. Note that the first field uses CURS ID# 4, which doesn't exist in the Finder. This field actually calls a cursor from the System file. There is one cursor in the System file so that all applications can call it, not just the Finder. That way, even if the application doesn't have an animated cursor sequence, it can call up this resource to indicate it is busy.

CREATING YOUR OWN WATCH CURSOR

Creating your own watch cursor involves several steps. The first steps are to create the cursors which will be used. Use the **Create New Resource...** menu command to create new frames for editing.

The next step is to create a new acur resource which will create the animation. Again, use **Create New Resource...** to get an acur resource. Make sure that the acur resource has the same ID number as the original acur resource from the application you are editing. When you wish to make new fields to enter new frames, click once on a row of asterisks within the editor itself, and choose **Insert New Field** to make a new field. This way, you can have as many frames as possible.

Cursor Animator: A Quick Alternative

It can be very time consuming to edit watch cursors. Even if you edit the Finder's watch cursor to something you really like, you may open an application to discover that is has its own animated sequence. This means that you have to edit this one as well.

There is a very good shareware program which will allow you to load cursors into memory, and then replace all watch cursors with the same animation sequence. To use it, you have to have two things in a resource file: the necessary CURS resources and the acur resource. The program (which is accessed through the Contol Panel) will then give you the option of opening this file. When you open the file, Cursor Animator shows you a name, which is chosen from the acur resource. As a result, you need to have an acur resource even if you're adding a non-animated cursor, so that your cursor will have a name.

Menus and You

by Steve Yaste

Chapter 6

Menus are one of the most visible attributes of a Macintosh program. It is through the menu structure that nearly all the functionality of a properly designed Macintosh program is reached.

With this much commonality between all programs, it is important to the Macintosh philosophy that Menus have a consistent *look and feel* for users. That is the reason all programs are mandated (in Apple's "Human Interface Design Guidelines") to have, as their first three Menus, the ⬝, **File**, and **Edit** Menus. Further, there are defined menu items which must appear in these menus (such as **Quit**, or **Undo**).

However, these menus can be boring. Every Macintosh menu looks basically the same. 12 pt. Chicago type in a long column running down the page. Sometimes it would be nice to have a variety of colors, or some icons. *ResEdit* allows you to make many interesting changes to a menu. Use *ResEdit* to open a copy of the *Finder*, and look at the menus which are there.

Figure 1 - The MENU resources within the Finder

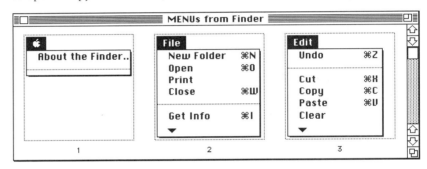

The MENU editor

Figure 2 - The Special menu in the Finder

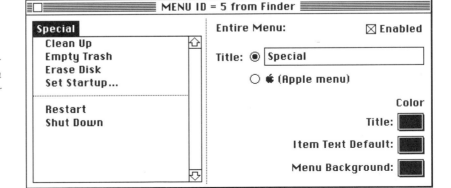

The above illustration shows the menu editor for MENU ID = 5 from the *Finder*. Looking over this window, we see the currently selected menu, and the items in it. The selected element (either the menu name or individual item) is highlighted. In this sample, the Menu Name is **Special**, and six menu items are listed.

The right hand side of the MENU editor shows the details of the selected resource item. In the case of this sample, the entire menu has been selected. The "Enabled" check-box allows you to specify whether the menu should initially be displayed as grayed-out (disabled) or normal. Below that, you can see the Title field with the Apple Menu radio button. These allow a person to easily specify a menu resource in his or her application as the Apple Menu, or to give it the name which will be used in the program.

On color systems, the menu color controls are below. You can individually specify different colors for the Menu Title, Item Text, and Menu Background. The menu background color only affects the backgrounds of individual menus, not the menu bar itself. Also note that the Item Text color is a default and will affect each of the menu's items; however, you can override these defaults for any particular menu item.

If you have ResEdit open now, you can see that the menu you are working on appears as the last item in the menubar, highlighted by a rectangle. Selecting this menu will allow you to see how the current menu will look to the user.

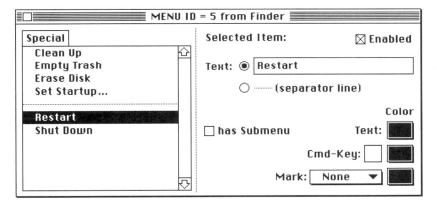

Figure 3 - The Restart menu option in the Special menu

In this illustration we see the same MENU resource, but we have now selected one of the menu items, and we see that a few things have changed. The editor now says "Selected Item" rather than "Entire Menu". Now that you have selected an item, all the changes made in the template will effect that menu item only. As in the case of the editing the entire menu, individual menu items may be grayed out as well. The Title box has changed to the Item Text box, and the radio button allows you to define this item as a separator line. (Separator lines can also be defined by entering a '-' as the item text.)

One very useful field in this editor is the "Cmd-Key" field. This allows you to set which command-key you would like to be associated with that particular menu item. Command-keys can often speed up work and productivity.

On color machines, there are controls for the colors of the menu item which has been selected.

By now, you are no doubt wondering when I'm going to get to the subject of icons. Let's look again at the **Special** menu from the *Finder*. The command for attaching an icon to a menu item is found in the **MENU**

Chapter 6
Menus and You

menu of ResEdit, in the MENU editor. Select the **Choose Icon...** item and you will be presented with the following dialog. *Note: When working on the Finder, you should be aware that an unaltered Finder won't have any ICON resources in it. You'll need to import some or create them in order to get icons.*

The **Choose Icon** dialog works with three types of ICON resources. ICONs, reduced ICONs, and SICNs. ICONs are resource types that date back to the original Macintosh resource set. Reduced icons are exactly the same as ICONs, except that the original 32x32 bit ICON is reduced to a 16x16 size. SICN's on the other hand, are relatively new Resource types which are designed to allow the developer to have more control over the appearance of the smaller 16x16 size ICON. You will select between which of these three ICON types you want to use in your program by selecting one of the three radio buttons on the left side of the window. *In order for ResEdit to use an icon for a menu, it must have an ID number between 257 and 511. Reset this as needed with the Get Info... dialog box under the* **Resource** *menu.*For now, just select the Normal Icons radio button. Just to the right of the radio buttons you will see four control buttons: NEW, EDIT, OK and CANCEL. OK and CANCEL function the same way, and the NEW and EDIT buttons are related to the icons themselves. Both of these buttons will show the ICON editor, either blank (for new icosn) or filled with the icon (for editing icons). *For more information about how to use this editor, see the ICON section earlier in this book.* Once you have completed your editing, select the OK button to save the ICON into the MENU. Again, you can see how your menu will look by pulling down the sample menu at the far right of the menubar in the MENU editor. If you wish to edit this ICON further at some later date you may either edit it from the MENU editor, or by opening and selecting the proper ICON resource directly. Please note that if you select the Reduced Icon radio button and then Edit, you will actually be editing the full sized version of the selected ICON.

If you later decide that you no longer want to have an Icon associated with your menu item, simply re-open the proper menu resource, select the menu item with the icon you wish to delete and select **Remove Icon** from the **MENU** menu.

More Technical Stuff:
Submenus and the rest of the MENU menu

When Apple introduced System 5.0, the Human Interface Design group added the ability to have hierarchical menus in your applications and on the Desktop. Many people have seen hierarchical menus in their favorite word processors or paint programs (Figure 5). While you won't be able to add functional sub-menus to your favorite commercial applications, you will be able to use ResEdit to easily define them for any applications you write.

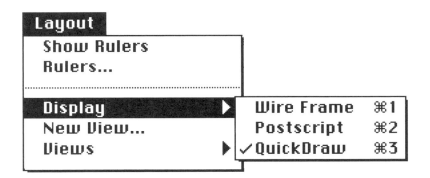

Figure 5 -
A menu with a
submenu attached to it.

If you look again at Figure 3, you will see that there is a checkbox next to the words "Has Submenu." If this box is not checked, there is no submenu for this item. If this checkbox is set, however, a new field will appear: "ID:" To use a submenu for a menu, you must enter the ID number of the menu resource you wish to use as the submenu. If you have not defined this submenu, you must be sure to enter an ID# that is unique from any other menu ID#'s you have defined. Defining the items for this sub-menu is done exactly the same way as defining items for a primary menu. Notice that when you create this new Menu ID# (*use CMD-I to assign the correct ID# if the sub-menu was not assigned the next available ID#*) it will be assigned the name of it's parent item (or a shortened version) as its ID name. In order to help keep things straight, it is recommended that you not change this title, even though your new title can only be seen with *ResEdit*.

There are a couple of useful things you should know about editing submenus. If you're looking at a menu item which uses a submenu, you can double-click on the menu item (within the list on the left-hand side) to bring the submenu forward. This can be handy if you wish to look at the submenu quickly. Another aspect of submenus is that command-key equivalents can not be assigned to menu items with submenus. This makes sense for two main reasons. First, what would happen if they did have a command-key equivalent? When a user used the command key, what would the application do? Show the submenu? Second, there is no room for the command-key on the right side of the menu. For these reasons, *ResEdit* will not even present the "Cmd-Key" field to you if the checkbox next to "Has Submenu" is checked.

Please note that some applications are dependent on menu items not changing positions, so be warned that if you move all your items around, your program may no longer function properly, if at all.

Occasionally when creating a program, you might wish to re-order the menu items so that their order makes more sense. I should point out that menu items can very easily be re-ordered merely by selecting the item you want to move, and holding down the mouse button, drag the menu item to its new position.

The **MENU** menu can also be used to return any MENU or Menu Item to the default black and white color scheme by selecting the menu title or menu item and then choosing the **Use Default Colors** menu item. The last item to discuss in this Menu is the **Edit Menu & MDEF ID...** item. This will bring up a new dialog which allow you to enter a new resource ID number and a new MDEF (Menu DEFinition) number. Each MENU resource has two ID#s. One is the resource ID# that we have already talked about and is generally assigned by *ResEdit* when you create a new menu resource. The second is the MDEF ID number set inside the menu editor. This number is only used by the Toolbox Menu management routines, and while it is not required that they be the same, life will certainly be easier if they are.

The MDEF number is generally '0' which is the number of the default System MDEF Proc, the standard pull-down menu. The only time that this might be different is when your application has non-standard menus such as palettes or ICON bars. Unless you are writing a program and have created unique, non-standard menu definitions, it is highly recommended that you not alter this ID#.

What can I do with these resources?

That is the theoretical information behind menus. What sort of practical applications can these be used for? One of the most useful is adding command-key equivalents to commonly-used menu items. Unfortunately, software companies can not anticipate the needs of every single person who uses their product. As a result, a menu command which you frequently use may not have a command key to activate it. You are then forced to mouse around to the menu and the menu item. With ResEdit, however, you can quickly assign a command key, as described above. When doing this, you should be careful about assigning a command key which is used somewhere else in the program. Make sure to investigate all the menus to determine their command key equivalents.

Although icons in menus may seem frivolous, they can be a valuable educational tool. If a person is not sure what a certain menu item does, a well-designed icon next to the command can get rid of a lot of confusion.

This is especially useful if you are creating *HyperCard* stacks with *Hyper-Card 2.0*. In the new version of this program, you can create menus and then insert them into the menubar when needed.

With these tools, you can do quite a bit to customize your menus to suit your own needs and the needs of others.

Chapter 6
Menus and You

Changing The Scroll Bar Pattern

by Derrick Schneider

Chapter 7

Patterns are one of the more subtle of the resources in the Macintosh system. They are always there, yet most people never notice them consciously. The average Mac user has his or her background pattern set to gray (which is the default) and never thinks twice about it. Most people don't even notice the pattern in the scroll bars, since it's always there and can't be changed with the Control Panel (like the background pattern can). For those people who do change the pattern on the desktop, most are content with the patterns which Apple provides. These patterns do provide some variety, but not much.

Look at the scroll bars on your Mac. Not bad, right? They've got a nice mellow pattern, and the arrows are fairly self-explanatory. Now think about how long you've had your Mac. In all that time, you've been looking at those exact same scroll bars, day in and day out. Wouldn't it be great if you could edit them in some way? How about a really cool, psychedelic pattern between those arrows? That would add a little bit of spice to your Macintosh, wouldn't it?

Since you'll be working with information which is stored in the System file, work on a copy. Make this with the **Duplicate** command in the Finder's **File** menu. Move this copy off your disk, as the Macintosh does not like having two Systems on one disk.

Open up *Copy of System* and open up the PAT resource. Note that the PAT resource has a space at the end of it. This can be very important if you are creating your own programs. Once you've opened this, you'll be seeing at least three PAT resources. PAT #16 is the desktop pattern, which you can return to later.

Figure 2 - The PAT s from the System

The PAT Editor

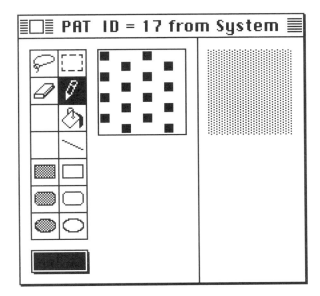

Figure 3 -
The PAT editor, with
the orginal pattern for
scroll bars displayed

Open up PAT #17, which is the scroll bar pattern. You should see something which looks like Figure 3. There is a tool area which features all the paint tools which are covered in "A Quick Review of the Paint Tools." There is a pattern palette which can be exposed by clicking on the black rectangle below the tools and holding the button down. This palette can then be "torn off" like those in *HyperCard*. The area on the left contains the editing panel. The area on the right shows you a small square which is filled with the actual pattern you are creating in the editing panel. With these tools you can create complex patterns. Do all your work on the left-hand panel. Figure 4 shows one pattern you can make.

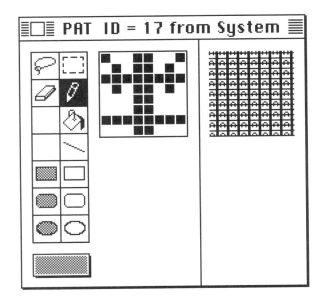

Figure 4 -
The PAT which I
created

To get a better idea of what your pattern looks like, choose Try Pattern from the PAT menu in the PAT editor. This will make your desktop pattern into the pattern which you are making.

Now here's where the creativity comes in. Play around with the pattern for a little while, and then save your changes when you get something you like. Remember that you're working on *Copy of System*, not the currently active System. Since the Mac uses the PAT s in the active System, it doesn't know about the changes you made to *Copy of System*. When you feel comfortable with the steps outlined here, you can go to work on the active System. The stuff you're doing with this resource won't blow up your computer or erase your hard drive. While it is good policy to work on a copy in many cases, it doesn't matter a lot for this particular resource. Keep in mind that that only applies to this particular resource. Also, do not delete any of these resources, as this will probably cause a system crash of some sort.

Other Stuff

Okay, you've managed to successfully change the patterns in the scroll bars. The adventuresome among you can try some other changes. Look at the other two PAT resources in your System file. One is #-15808 and the other is #16. PAT #16 controls the background pattern (if you've got a desktop picture, opening this might look kind of strange, but it still applies; the background is covered by the picture) and PAT #-15808 controls the pattern which fills up empty space in the control panel (if you don't know what this means, go to the Mouse cdev in the control panel and you'll get an idea). Experiment with changes you can make in these.

There are actually four types of pattern resources in the System. We have already discussed the PAT resource. The PAT# resource represents the patterns available to a program. For instance, when you use the Control Panel to change the desktop pattern, you may notice that you can choose certain pre-designed patterns. These are the PAT#s in the System. For those of you who are lucky enough to have color Macintoshes, there are two additional resources which you can play with. The ppat resources perform the same function as the PAT resource, except in color. This allows one to create desktop patterns. The ppt# resource works exactly like the PAT# resource, again in color. Experiment with these for a while to come up with aesthetic combinations.

All About Fonts

by Jens Peter Alfke

The Macintosh font system is a fine example of the phenomenon called thin ice. The friendly surface world of fonts, with its little pictures of suitcases and jolly names like BenguBolIta, is rather fragile. Poking too hard at it, putting too much weight on it, or just stepping in the wrong place, can send you crashing down into the depths; and the depths are much more complicated than the surface.

In the olden days of computers, rescue from below the ice was effected by shambling, superhuman programmers, who would stare at hex dumps, quaff mightily from tankards of cola, and patch your operating system until it spat you back out onto the surface. Today, in the have-a-nice-day world of the Mac, we have friendly programs with jack-in-the-box icons that give the same powers to non-programmers. At the risk of placing a dangerous amount of weight on my thin-ice metaphor, this article explains how to use a saw, wet-suit and scuba gear. It also describes some of the murky terrain of the river-bed. It is *not* a travelogue of the happy surface world; there are many good books and magazine articles that provide that. Let's dive!

Macintosh fonts (see below for information about PostScript fonts) are divided into four main types of resources. Each one is discussed briefly below.

FONT

Sensibly-named, the FONT resource was the original font system introduced with the 128K Macintosh. With this resource, each size of font is stored in a different resource. Thus, Times 18 and Times 14 were two separate FONT resources. In this system, every typeface also includes a special FONT resource, which serves as a divider. It has no size, but its name is the name of the font. Thus, when you open a FONT resource, you'll see several resources which take up no space. This special resource is used to store the name of the typeface. These resource names are the ones which actually end up displayed in applications' Font menus. All the Macintosh System fonts are still done this way, as are many other bitmap fonts.

FOND

Once the LaserWriter came on the scene and users started trying to produce real typography on the desktop, some substantial limits with FONTs became apparent. One of these limitations arose from the fact that there is no provision for typeface families, with true bolds and italics and the like. If you italicized some Times text, all that happened on-screen was that the Macintosh slanted the regular Times. If you emboldened it, the Macintosh smeared the original to make it darker. As real typography, these tricks just don't work. In addition to this, the widths of characters in a FONT are specified in points (or pixels) so every character had to be an integral number of pixels wide. However, real characters don't have such even widths, so round-off error was inevitable. This translated into badly-spaced text, since the Mac's and the LaserWriter's ideas of line widths came out different. (You will still run into this problem if you don't turn on your word-processor's "Fractional Widths" setting.)

The solution was a new resource to contain the extra information needed: the FOND, for FONt Definition. There is one FOND resource for each typeface. Its resource id is the same as the font ID, and its name is the name of the typeface. The information in the FOND includes:

- High-resolution equivalents of values previously stored in FONT resources, such as the font ascent, descent and linespacing, and character widths. These are fractional values that can be scaled to any point-size.

- Flags related to PostScript printing; these mostly tell what to do if some styles, such as a true bold or italic, are missing.

- A Font Association Table (FAT), which lists the resource IDs of FONTs (and NFNTs) to use for various point-sizes and styles (see below).

```
┌──────────────────────────────────────────────────────────┐
│ ▣▢▨▨▨▨▨▨ FOND "Chicago" ID = 0 from System ▨▨▨▨ │
│ International                                          ⇧  │
│ I                                                        │
│ FOND version  │$0002        │                            │
│ # of Font      0                                         │
│ entries                                                  │
│   1) *****                                               │
│     Font Size     │ 12        │                          │
│     Font Style    │ 0         │                          │
│     Res ID        │ 12        │                          │
│   2) *****                                               │
│ The Tables  $│                            │          ⇩  │
└──────────────────────────────────────────────────────────┘
```

- A style table, which lists the PostScript font names to use for different styles. This is how the Mac tells the LaserWriter what fonts to use, and how it finds downloadable PostScript font files to send the LaserWriter.

- Kerning tables for one or more styles.

NFNT

Even using FONDs, the font system was still limited as long as FONTs were used. Because of their odd numbering scheme, there was still only a tiny range of font ids: from 0 to 255. This meant, of course, that no one could have more than 256 typefaces, including the ubiquitous Chicago and Geneva, installed at a time. Also, if there were more than 256 Macintosh typefaces, some of them would undoubtedly have the same IDs. This limit was quickly reached, even before PostScript typefaces became widely available. *Font/DA Mover* tries to help. If you copy a new font into your System file, but the System already contains a different font with the same ID number, the incoming font will be renumbered as it's installed. This results in different sets of ID numbers on different Macs, the inevitable result being that your co-worker's document, set in New York, would appear in Courier on your Mac.

The solution to this numbering problem was to fix the numbering scheme. This required using a new resource type (to avoid numbering conflicts with FONTs) even though the data inside stayed the same. Thus the NFNT, for New FoNT, or New Font Numbering Table was born. NFNTs contain the same data as FONTs, but since they are referenced only through Font Association Tables, they can have arbitrary resource ids. When copying fonts, the *Font/DA Mover* will renumber individual NFNT resources (updating the FAT references) to make sure that no two in the same file have the same id. This renumbering causes no harm to documents, since NFNT IDs are used only by the internals of the Font Manager.

Freed of the 256-font limit, typefaces can have font IDs up to 16,383 — as long as the bitmap fonts are contained in NFNT resources. (The range from 16,384 to 32,767 is reserved by the Script Manager for fonts of other writing systems such as Hebrew or Kanji.) Apple registered font IDs, making sure that no two fonts, even from different vendors, had the same ID. Everything seemed fine until mid-1990, when it came to pass that the entire range was used up. Now we're back in the same boat: there will be different fonts with the same ids, and as a result different people's systems may have different ids for the same fonts.

sfnt

The sfnt is the latest addition to the family. To be introduced in System 7, sfnts are outline fonts, just like PostScript fonts. This means that they contain mathematical descriptions (known as *spline curves*) of the outlines of characters. System 7's TrueType technology can scale these outlines up to any point size and fill them in with pixels, allowing for smooth, well-shaped characters at large point-sizes. This is a skill which bitmap fonts, such as those controlled by the FONT resource, sorely lack, as anyone knows who's tried to type in a size which is not available. The sfnt resource provides the same immediate advantages as *Adobe Type Manager*. They are better integrated into the system, making them easier to install and

A B C...

more amenable to future growth. No separate downloadable PostScript font is required; the sfnt resource lives in suitcase files or the System, just as other font resources do.

What's In a Font

A font or typeface (the two terms have become almost interchangeable) is a set of images of characters. Since the characters are intended to be placed next to one another in a line, it includes not only the shape of each character, but its vertical alignment, relative to the baseline, and horizontal spacing, relative to adjacent characters. (The alignment and spacing are called *metrics*.)

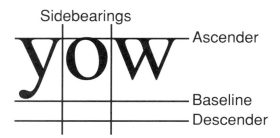

There is also information that applies globally to all the characters, such as the *leading* — the distance between lines of type in a font. Technically, leading is the amount of extra space between lines plus the point size, measured from the baseline of one line to the baseline of the next line. For example, 12pt. type with 14pt. space between lines (often called 12/14) has 2pts. of leading.

Also, a font may have a table of *kern pairs*, which are adjustments to the spacing between specific pairs of characters, such as "A" and "V".

And, of course, every font or typeface has a name.

Beyond these attributes, there is also an internal set of linkages that connect fonts to one another. In the old days of just the FONT resource, there had to be a linkage between different sizes and styles of the same typeface. When you change text to 18pt. Times Bold, the Font Manager within the Macintosh can follow these linkages to find the appropriate set of bitmaps to display.

Editing Font Resources

Of all the different font resource types, only the FONT has a graphic editor. You can modify an existing FONT with ease, and create new fonts with slightly less ease.

The FONT editor has several important components. As with all bitmap editors, the largest part of the editor is a FatBits view of the character you will be editing (in this case, the letter 'A' in Figure 4). To choose a

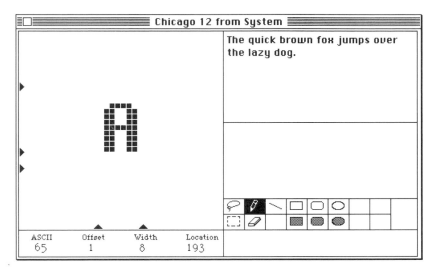

The quick brown fox jumps over
the lazy dog.

ASCII	Offset	Width	Location
65	1	8	193

Figure 4 –
When editing FONTs
on a color Macintosh,
be sure to set the
monitor to black and
white while you work.
If the monitor is in a
color mode, the FONT
editor will not work
perfectly.

different character, simply click it on your keyboard. The two upward-pointing triangles on either side of the character mark the left and right sidebearings of the character – its left and right margins. Dragging these outward increases the amount of space around the character, dragging them inward reduces it. It is perfectly alright for the character to stick out past the sidebearings on either side; this means that it will overhang neighboring characters. Many italic letters do this.

The baseline marker shows the baseline. The line on which all characters in a line, regardless of font, size or style, sit. It cannot be moved.

The ascender and descender lines are the two small arrows on the left side of the editing area (ascender is the top arrow) and mark the top and bottom of the entire font. No part of the font can go above the ascender or below the descender. (If you move these markers too far in, you will end up chopping off the tops or bottoms of letters. Be careful!) The ascender and descender are also used to determine the linespacing of the font, but modern applications get this information from the FOND or make it up themselves.

Below the editing area are some numeric displays. These show more-or-less technical information that will probably not be of much use to the more casual user. The ASCII code is the internal code (0–255) of the character. The offset is the distance from the leftmost black pixel to the leftmost left-side-bearing marker of the entire font (sorry you asked?); the width is the set width of the character (the amount the "pen" moves when drawing that character, equal to the distance between the left and right sidebearing markers); and the location is the offset to the character's bitmap in the font's internal storage.

Finally, there is a sample text display at the top right, so you can see how the characters look in context. If your screen is not in color or grayscale mode, any changes you make to the characters will be reflected in

A B
C ...

Chapter 8
All About Fonts

the sample text. You can edit the sample text by clicking on it; then you can type, or drag to select text, as in any other text field. Clicking outside the text box removes the selection or insertion point. From then on, typing will switch the currently edited character. This same editor is used by the NFNT resource. Thus, NFNTs can be edited just like FONTs.

The FOND editor

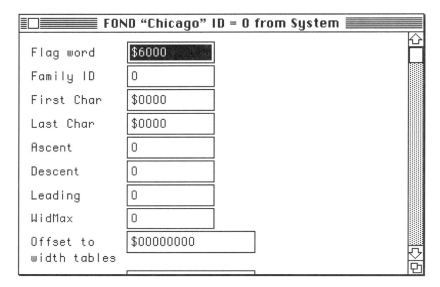

Despite the fact that most of the blanks are in hexadecimal, *ResEdit* will allow you to type in decimal numbers. Most of the fields should remain undisturbed, but some can be very useful. For instance, several fields allow you to set extra widths for different styles (bold, italic, etc.). The FOND resource also has fields which can be used to set global values for the ascender and descender of a character, no matter what the size. Near the end of the FOND resource (directly before the field labeled "The Tables"), one can find the Font Association Table—the FAT.

The FAT lists the resource ids of screen fonts (FONTs, NFNTs and even sfnts) to use for various point-sizes and styles within a FOND. Thus, when the computer needs a new size for a font (e.g., if you wish to make your report look bigger by changing to 14 point instead of 12 point), it looks to the FAT area of the FOND resource so that it knows what FONT, NFNT, or sfnt to use for that size and style. By including style information, it makes it possible to have real screen fonts for italic and bold styles. If you add new point-sizes to a typeface, or create a new bitmap typeface,If you wish to add a new section to the FAT, click on a row of asterisks before "The Tables," and choose Insert New Field from the Resource menu.

The FAT is a typical ResEdit list. Each entry in the list consists of a point-size, a style code, and the resulting resource id. The point size is the actual size of the font you are referring to. The style code is the result of adding together various style values:

1	Bold
2	Italic
4	Underline
8	Outline
16	Shadow
32	Condensed
64	Extended
256	4-color font
512	16-color font
768	256-color font

Following this formula, Bold Condensed style would be 1 (Bold) + 32 (Condensed) = 33. In practice, only the Bold and Italic bits, and sometimes Condensed and Extended, are used.

NFNTs are accessed through the FAT and can be given any resource IDs, so long as those ids don't conflict with any other NFNTs. A FONT resource can't be given a different id just because it's being referenced through a FAT. It must still use the 128*_font id_ + _size_ formula. (For this reason a typeface that uses any FONT resources cannot have a font id greater than 255.)

If you renumber FONT or NFNT resources associated with a font, you must update the entries in the FAT. And if you add or delete sizes by hand, you must keep the FAT up to date or the Font Manager won't see the changes.

It's very important that the entries in the FAT remain sorted. The point-sizes are listed in increasing order, and within a point-size the style codes are listed in increasing order. If you don't do this you will seriously annoy the Font Manager, and it will return many kinds of wonderful System Errors.

ResEdit does not currently support editors for either NFNTs. However, there are several shareware and commercial utilities which do. One of these is FontMaster 88, which is available from most online services and user groups.

ResEdit will possibly support editors for sfnts, as they become more widely used in System 7.

Renaming or Renumbering a FOND

In all modern Macintoshes, it is the FOND resource which gives a typeface its name and font id. (Some old suitcase files may contain raw FONTs without a FOND, but _Font/DA Mover_ will add the necessary FOND when it copies those FONTs into another file.)

If you wish to rename the typeface, all you have to do is use the

Get Resource Info… command to change the resource name . Keep in mind that all applications (such as *PageMaker*) that store font names in documents will no longer recognize the font name in existing documents, and will probably change the type to Geneva or Courier.

To renumber a typeface, change the resource number of the FOND. Then open the FOND and change the "Family ID" field to the new number. (If all the bitmaps for the typeface are stored in NFNTs, Apple suggests you use a new font id in the range 256–1023, since that range is reserved for renumbered typefaces.)

If some of the bitmaps for this typeface are stored in FONT resources, you'll have to renumber all the FONTs since their numbering is based on the font id. For each FONT, compute the new resource number based on the new font id. Renumber the FONT resource accordingly, and change the resource number stored in the FAT.

Renumbering incurs the same problem as renaming; applications that rely on font ids will lose references to the font stored in existing documents.

For people who use *Microsoft Word*: Never renumber the Symbol font if you plan on using Word's formula commands. Word assumes that the Symbol font's id is 23 when it displays math characters in formulas. If this is no longer true, you will get garbage characters, most likely in Geneva, in your formulas.

Inside PostScript Font Files

Downloadable PostScript font files aren't usually very interesting or informative to look at, but I'll describe them here for the benefit of those of you who simply must know everything. These files are just containers for the PostScript code that makes up a downloadable font. When a document being printed to a PostScript printer makes use of a PostScript font that isn't already living inside the printer, the Mac looks (by name) for a downloadable file for that font. Then, it sends the enclosed PostScript code to the printer. The result is that the font is now living inside the printer and can be printed.

Those Weird File Names

The file names of downloadable PostScript fonts are a great source of amusement to nearly everyone. They're also very important, as you will agree if you've ever renamed one and then tried to print with that font.

When the Mac looks for a downloadable file for a particular font, it looks for it by the name of the PostScript font. Unfortunately, Macintosh filenames can't be longer than 31 characters, and some PostScript font names can exceed that limit. So the name of the downloadable font file is compacted. It uses the first five letters of the first word of the font name, and the first three letters of each following word. (This is called the 5-3-3 rule.) Thus, the PostScript font called "BenguiatGothic-BoldItalic" resides in a downloadable file called "BenguGotBolIta".

What's Inside

Downloadable files contain only a few resources. Most, such as the BNDL, FREF, and ICN#, are just there to give the file its icon in the Finder. All the PostScript code is contained in POST resources.

The POST resources start with number 501 and increase from there. Each resource contains a flag byte, another byte of filler, and then the data. (The template provided by ResEdit is wrong. When you open POST resources, use the Open Using Hex Editor command to open them. Then you'll just get a hex dump.)

If the flag byte is 1, the rest of the data is plain text. POST 501 is almost always of this variety. The following text is the PostScript font header, which contains some interesting stuff like the PostScript font name, the font type (1 or 3) and the copyright notice.

Most of the succeeding resources have a flag byte of 2, which indicates compressed binary data. This is basically unintelligible to the human eye.

The last resource will have a flag of 5, which indicates the end of the data.

Some fonts have a POST resource with a flag of 3: this means that the rest of the PostScript data is in the data fork of the file, and isn't stored in resources at all.

Creating New FONTs

To create a new size of an existing typeface, open up a suitcase containing all current sizes of that typeface, with screen fonts stored as FONTs, not NFNTs. Open the FONT resource picker and use the Create New Resource command. Choose the appropriate typeface from the scrolling list, type in the point-size, and press OK. A FONT editor will open for your new screen-font.

Before you do anything else, drag the ascender up and the descender down enough to make room for drawing. Otherwise nothing will show up. Then you can draw each character, making sure to move the sidebearings apart so the characters don't overlap.

Very Important: After you're done, open the FOND and add a FAT entry for your new FONT. If you don't do this, the Font Manager won't find it.

Uses for Bitmap fonts

There are still a few uses left for new all-bitmap typefaces. One of the common uses for these fonts is in HyperCard stacks, as aids in animation. Since the author of a stack can change the contents of a field, it is possible to use a font for animation. To do this, create your new font (see above) in a separate file, and use *ResEdit* to paste the font and FOND resources into the stack. Working in a separate file prevents any damage which might affect the stack you are working on. Once you're in *HyperCard*, use the scripting commands to change the characters in your "animation field." The

AB C...

field will look like there is animated artwork inside, even though you're simply typing stuff in from behind the scenes.

Another use for the font resources is to add a character to a font. If you have a certain character which you would like to use, and it isn't in a font, you can just add it to the appropriate FONT resource (if the font is held in a FONT resource, like the Macintosh System fonts). Keep in mind that since each FONT represents one size, the special character will only be available in that size. To use it in all the sizes, you will have to add it to each separate FONT resource.

Another possible use for the font resources is to add a new size to an existing font. This may take some time, but it can be worth it if a font which you really like does not come in a desired size.

Changing Your Keyboard Layout

By James W. Walker

Recently I've seen several questions, on CompuServe and the Internet, about remapping keyboards.

Q: How do you keep the period and comma keys from changing with the Shift key, instead of turning into "<" and ">"? The person who asked this question owns *Tempo II*, which didn't help and was also incompatible with *MacroMaker*. He could have bought *QuicKeys*, but of course that costs money.

Q: How do you exchange the functions of the Control and Shift keys?

Q: How do you remap the keyboard to the Dvorak configuration (a keyboard layout for English that is said to allow more efficient typing)?

Q: How do you make the Shift and Caps Lock keys cancel each other out? That is, when you have the Caps Lock key down and you want to type a occasional lowercase letter, you might like the Shift key to switch you back into lowercase.

Q: How do you disable the Caps Lock key? Some people rarely use the CapsLock key, but often hit it accidentally.

All of these problems can be solved by using *ResEdit* to create or modify a keyboard mapping resource called a KCHR.

Each key on your keyboard, whether it's a character key or a modifier key such as Shift, has a numerical "raw key code." The *System* uses a table called a KMAP to translate the raw key code into a "virtual key code." For most keys, the virtual key code is the same as the raw key code. (When I simply say "key code," I will mean virtual key code.) *ResEdit* does not have an editor for KMAPs, and I would not advise altering them.

After a keystroke has been translated to virtual key codes, it is translated to a character using a KCHR resource. A KCHR resource contains several translation tables. Each combination of modifiers activates one of these tables, but a table may serve more than one combination of modifiers. Since there are five modifier keys (Shift, Option, Command, Control, and CapsLock) there are 32 possible combinations of modifiers, so there could be up to 32 tables in a KCHR. However, the standard U.S. KCHR has only 8 translation tables. For instance, translation table 0 is used for no modifier, or for Command, or for Command-Shift.

If you have more than one KCHR installed in your system, you can use the *Keyboard* Control Panel Device (which comes with the system software) to choose between these different keyboard layouts. This is seen in Figure 1. Note the small icons to the left of each keyboard layout. Every KCHR can have an SICN associated with it. *The author of this article has supplied a file for the disk, called KCHR resources. It contains many sample KCHRs you can paste into your own system and use.*

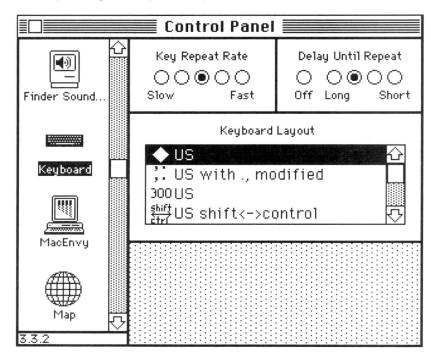

*Figure 1 -
The Control Panel,
opened to the Key-
board cdev, showing a
list of KCHRs installed
in the System.*

The KCHR Editor

Figure 2 is a KCHR as displayed by *ResEdit*. At the time this snapshot was taken, the Command and Option keys were pressed. This caused those keys to be highlighted in the keyboard layout diagram at the bottom, and caused the appropriate translation table, Table 6, to be displayed.

In the upper left of the picture, there is a table of the ASCII character set, laid out in a 16x16 array. This array cannot be changed, except for the font and size. However, when you press a key, the character to which it is mapped will highlight in the character array. You can also drag characters from the character array to one of the other arrays, as discussed later.

To the immediate right of the character array is a 16x8 array. The positions in this array represent key codes. The character at a given position is the one that corresponds to the key code, when a particular table is active. For instance, in the picture above, Table 6 has an infinity sign in the eighth row and second column. This means that the keycode $17 (that's hexadecimal) gets translated to the infinity character when the Command and Option keys are pressed.

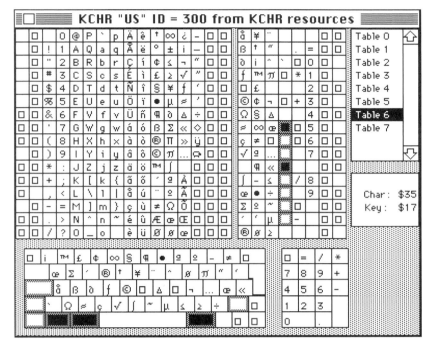

Figure 2 -
The KCHR editor

Remapping Ordinary Keys

Let's say we want to make Shift-period send a period instead of a greater-than sign. Find the period in the character array by pressing the period key. This will highlight the period key in the character array. Press and hold the Shift key. Click the mouse on the period in the character array and drag it to the place you want it on the keyboard, i.e., right on top of the greater-than sign in the keyboard diagram. Release the mouse, then release the Shift key. That's it! What you've done here is held down the Shift key to tell *ResEdit* that you wish to have access to the translation table corresponding to the Shift key. Then, when you move the period to its new location, you're making sure that a Shift-period will send this character. Note that when you let go of the Shift key (and return to the normal translation table), the period is still where it should be. This is because you have only modified the period key with the Shift key held down.

Remapping Modifier Keys

Recall that the various tables shown in the KCHR window correspond to certain combinations of modifier keys. The US KCHR has eight tables. Experimentation reveals the correlation shown in Figure 3.

Chapter 9
Key Layout

Table	Modifiers
0	none (also Command, Command-Shift, etc.)
1	Shift
2	CapsLock
3	Option
4	Shift-Option
5	CapsLock-Option
6	Command-Option
7	Control (also Control-Shift, Control-Option, etc.)

Figure 3 -
A simple chart which
will tell you which
combinations of
modifier keys belong to
which tables in the
U.S. KCHR resource.

Let's suppose we want to exchange the roles of the Shift and Control keys. This will require a number of table reassignments. For instance, to assign Table 1 to the Control key, hold down the Control key and click on Table 1 in the table list. *ResEdit* will show an alert asking if you really want to do this, as in Figure 4.

Figure 4 -
The Alert box asking
you if you wish to
replace the contents of
a translation table.

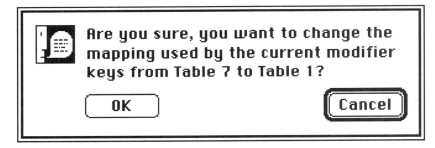

Are you sure, you want to change the mapping used by the current modifier keys from Table 7 to Table 1?

OK   Cancel

Click OK. You will also need to reassign Shift to Table 7, Control-Option to Table 4, Command-Control to Table 0, and so on.

I used this general technique to make the "No CapsLock" KCHR in *KCHR resources*. Since Figure 6 shows that two of the eight tables involve the CapsLock key, I expected to be able to use the Remove unused tables menu command to get rid of two tables. That proved a bit tricky, because several modifier key combinations other than CapsLock-Option were bound to Table 5. I had to uncouple the modifier keys (see below) and remove combinations like CapsLock-Option-(Right-hand Option).

Dead Keys

In the standard U.S. keyboard layout, there are five keystrokes called "dead keys" that behave in a special way, in order to place accents on other letters. They are Option-e, Option-i, Option-u, Option-n, and Option-grave accent. For instance, if you press Option-e, nothing happens, so the key seems "dead"; but if you then press o, you get an accented o, ó. Only certain letters can take an accent. If you follow Option-e by a letter that can't be accented, like x, you get an accent followed by an x. Typing Option-e twice produces the accent alone.

If you type a dead key while in the KCHR editor in *ResEdit*, it brings up a special dead key editing window, depicted in Figure 5. You can also use the **Edit Dead Key** command from the **KCHR** menu.

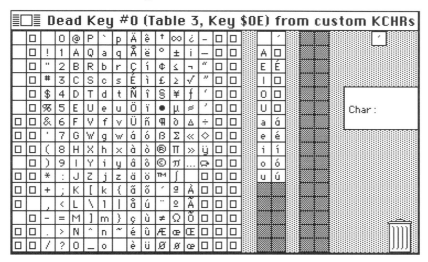

*Figure 5 -
The dead key editor.*

The biggest part of the dead key editing window is a character array, just like that in the main KCHR editing window. To the right of that, there is a list of pairs of characters. Each pair is simply the character without the accent and with the accent. The lone character near the upper right corner is the result of typing the dead key twice or following a dead key by a character for which you have not defined an accent.

For instance, let's say you want to define an accented x to be an infinity sign, for some reason. Drag an x from the character array to the left-hand spot of one of the unoccupied pairs, then drag an infinity character to the right-hand spot. If you change your mind, drag either of those characters from the pair list to the trash can.

To make the dead key into an ordinary key, just select Remove dead key from the KCHR menu

KCHRs and the International Mac

Keyboard layouts are controlled by the part of the Macintosh system called the Script Manager. The Script Manager is largely responsible for the Mac's ability to work with different languages and writing systems. Each writing system, or "script," has an identification number. For instance, the Roman script, used for most European languages, is number 0, Japanese is 1, Arabic is 4, and Vietnamese is 30.

Each script has a range of possible KCHR ID numbers. The Roman script gets the lion's share of potential KCHR ID numbers, 0 through 16383. Each other script has a range of 512 KCHR numbers, starting from 16384 + 512*(script number - 1).

For each script, there is a currently active KCHR. The KCHR for the next time the system starts up is stored in an "itlb" resource whose resource ID is the script number.

Naturally, foreign Macintosh systems are likely to have better facilities for dealing with scripts and keyboards than the U.S. version. For instance, in the Chinese version of *System 6.0.3*, one can toggle the keyboard between the Chinese and Roman scripts just by clicking on a small icon in the menu bar or by typing Command-space. However, to change KCHRs within a script, it is necessary to use the *Keyboard* control device.

Switching KCHRs Without the Control Panel

ResEdit can be used to change which keys are used to activate an FKEY. Simply change the ID number of the FKEY to another single digit. This digit is the new activation key.

I have included an FKEY called "switch KCHR" in the *KCHR resources* file. Once it is installed, you will be able to switch KCHRs by just pressing Command-Shift-7 rather than by using the *Control Panel*. Actually, switching KCHRs with the *Control Panel* does one thing that the FKEY does not: It sets the current KCHR as the startup KCHR.

The trouble with switching with an FKEY is that it gives no visual feedback. However, if you are running *System 6.0.5* or later, you can make the small icon of the active KCHR appear in the menu bar, just to the left of *MultiFinder's* application-switching SICN: Edit the "itlc" resource in the *System* file, and set the "Always show icon" flag to 1. Figure 6 shows this with the SICN for the standard U.S. KCHR.

Figure 6 - The small icon associated with the U.S. KCHR, shown in its position in the menubar

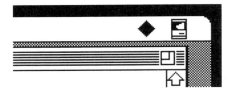

There is also an INIT/cdev on the disk called *Keyboard Switcher* which provides yet another way to switch KCHRs. It can display the keyboard SICN anywhere in the menu bar, and will run on systems earlier than 6.0.5 (but not *too* much earlier.) Clicking on the SICN rotates through the available KCHRs. If you option-click on the SICN, you get a menu of the names of the KCHRs. Switching KCHRs this way does not set the startup KCHR, but the *Keyboard Switcher* cdev does allow you to set the startup KCHR to be the same as the active KCHR. To use the program, drop it into your System Folder. *Note: If you use* Keyboard Switcher, *you don't need to paste the FKEY "switch KCHR" into your system.*

Uncoupling Modifier Keys

You might wonder about the item Uncouple modifier keys in the KCHR menu. This option allows the right-hand Shift, Option, and Control keys to be treated differently from their left-hand counterparts, at least on the Apple Extended keyboard. Quoting *Inside Macintosh*: "This capability is included for compatibility with certain existing operating systems that distinguish the left and right keys. Its use by new applications violates Apple user interface guidelines and is strongly discouraged."

Some Applications Won't Pay Attention to KCHRs

Some applications may read the keycodes, rather than the character codes, produced by the keyboard. For instance, I understand that *Page-Maker* uses the numeric keypad for certain operations. Since the numbers on the keypad generate the same character codes as the numbers along the top of the keyboard, *PageMaker* must be reading the key codes. Such keys cannot be remapped with a KCHR.

Associating SICNs with KCHRs

Earlier we discussed the fact that KCHRs can have a small icon (or SICN) associated with them. This is useful if you wish visual feedback about what keyboard layout you are using. If you are running *System 6.0.5* or later, you can display the small icon of the current KCHR in the menubar by modifying the itlb resource. Just set the "Always Show Icon" radio button to '1' or 'true.'

In order to attach an SICN to a KCHR, open the SICN resource in the *System*, and choose Create New Resource from the Resource menu. Edit the SICN until it looks the way you want. Now, give it the same ID number as the KCHR resource you want to attach it to. The system will associate the two resources.

What Can You Do With This?

The KCHR resource can be used for a wide variety of purposes. As this article discusses, it can be used to set up keyboard layouts which may be more comfortable to you. For instance, if you are accustomed to the Shift and Control keys being in a different location (if you use another computer at home or work, for instance), you can simply swap them.

One common use of the KCHR resource is to swap the positions of the plus and minus keys on the numeric keypad. This is especially useful to people who use adding machines, and are used to the plus sign being below the minus sign.

Another potential use is if you have a special character (such as one produced by holding down the Option key) which you use frequently. By adjusting the KCHR, you can replace a key you rarely use with the character you do.

The Overseas Mac

by Blaise R. Pabón

ResEdit has the power to modify programs to reflect differences in language and currency formats among users in foreign countries. Apple produces system software for many languages and provides built-in support for "localization," or adapting software for different cultural conventions. This support exists in the form of the international utilities package.

The international utilities package makes use of several resources. In the beginning, there was one resource type called 'INTL' which contained two resources with IDs 0 and 1. INTL 0 contained the symbols for local currency, date and time. INTL 1 contained the names of the months and the days of the week. INTL 1 also had a code which controlled alternative ordering sequences for sorting.

However, this created a problem when an application wished to suddenly switch to another local convention. As this was realized, Apple developed some new resources which were better equipped for switching quickly between different international setups. These new resource types were itl0 and itl1. At first, itl0 resources contain the same information, in the same format as INTL 0, and itl1s contained the same information as INTL 1.

By putting this information into separate resources, the Macintosh Operating System could support multiple sets of local conventions. An application may now switch date and currency formats within a single document.

ResEdit has complete editors for types INTL, ilt0 and itl1. The editors within older versions of ResEdit were rather cryptic but those included in this version of ResEdit are very straightforward. Like the other resource editors, they can be opened by double-clicking on the icon of the resource.

The itl0 Editor

The itl0 editor allows you to edit both the INTL 0 resource and all resources of type itl0. The editor is broken into three main sections: numbers, short date, and time. Each one has several controls and fields which you can fill in to give you complete flexability. When you alter one of the parameters in one of the sections, you will get immediate visual feedback due to the sample text in the lower left of each section. This is very useful for seeing how your changes look.

The "Number" section allows you to set the parameters for how numbers and currency are displayed. The four fields allow you to set the punctuation you wish to use as a decimal point, a thousands separator (as in 1,024), a list separator (when you have two values together), and a currency symbol. The checkboxes on the right allow even more customization. The "Leading Currency Symbol" determines whether or not the currency symbol is used at the beginning of the value or at the end. "Minus sign for negative" allows you to choose whether or not the minus sign is used for negative numbers. "Trailing decimal zeros" gives you the ability to decide whether or not you wish to have two zeros appear after a decimal point. "Leading integer zeros", when set to true, will place a zero before a decimal point if the value is less than one.

The "Short Date" section determines how the date will look when compressed into short date form (e.g. 12/7/70). With the pop-up menu, you can quickly switch between the six possible arrangements of year, month, and date in the short date. The "Date Separator" field can be filled with the character or characters of your choice, and this punctuation mark will appear between all the values of the date. "Leading 0 for day" places a zero in front of the date if it is less than 10. Similarly, "Leading 0 for month" will place a zero before the value for the month if it is before October (month number 10). "Include century" will force the entire year number to be placed in the short date (e.g., 1990 instead of 90).

The "Time" section has all the parameters needed for customizing the way in which time is displayed. As with the "Short Date" section, this section has a field which lets you choose the character you want to separate the hour value from the minutes. With the three other fields, you can set the way the System indicates AM, PM, or Greenwich Time. The checkboxes are mostly for leading zeros (see above). The fourth checkbox, however, allows you to determine whether or not the default is 12-hour time.

Finally, there is a pop-up menu featuring the country codes, which lets you determine what country code is associated with your custom setup.

itl0 "US" ID = 0 from System	
Numbers: Decimal Point: `.`	☒ **Leading Currency Symbol**
Thousands separator: `,`	☐ **Minus sign for negative**
($1,234.50) List separator: `;`	☒ **Trailing decimal zeros**
($0.5) ; ($0.5) Currency: `$`	☒ **Leading integer zero**
Short Date: Date separator: `/`	☐ **Leading 0 for day**
Date Order: `M/D/Y ▼`	☐ **Leading 0 for month**
11/14/90	☐ **Include century**
Time: Time separator: `:`	☒ **Leading 0 for seconds**
5:05:35 PM Morning trailer: `AM`	☒ **Leading 0 for minutes**
5:05:35 AM Evening trailer: `PM`	☐ **Leading 0 for hours**
24-hour trailer: ` `	☒ **12-hour time cycle**
Country: `00 - USA ▼`	☐ metric Version: `1`

The itl1 Editor

The itl1 resource contains the names of the months and the days of the week. These appear in boxes along the top half of the itl1 editor window. In the middle of the window there is a series of pop-up menus which allow you to change the sequence of day, month, date (the actual number in the month), and the year. These are separated by fields which can be used to indicate what sort of separators you want between all these values. In the lower left-hand corner there is a sample of the date written with the current parameters to provide you with feedback.

As with the itl0 editor, you can select which country code you wish to associate with this resource. There is also a field which lets you specify how many characters are used when abbreviating a month or a day. The checkboxes on the right side of the editor are mostly for suppressing various values in the date. When one of these boxes is checked, or set to true, that value will not be shown in the date. The "Leading 0 in Date" places a zero in front of integers less than ten.

itl1 "US" ID = 0 from System

Names for months

January	July
February	August
March	September
April	October
May	November
June	December

Names for days

| Sunday |
| Monday |
| Tuesday |
| Wednesday |
| Thursday |
| Friday |
| Saturday |

Day ▼ , Month ▼ Date ▼ , Year ▼

Use 3 characters to abbreviate names

Country Code: 00 - USA ▼

Wed, Nov 14, 1990   Version: 1
Wednesday, November 14, 1990

☐ Leading 0 in Date
☐ Suppress Date
☐ Suppress Day
☐ Suppress Month
☐ Suppress Year

How this all works

In order to deal with foreign systems, Apple developed the Script Manager. The Script Manager is a collection of routines in the Macintosh Toolbox that provide support for non-roman (other than American) writing systems. Arabic and KanjiTalk are two examples of conventions which are supported. Thus, applications which are Script Manager compatible will accept non-roman languages and print from right to left without modification. The Script Manager was implemented at about the time of System 4.1. After that, all Macs had the Script Manager built into their ROMs. This includes all Macs from the SE and up. The Script Manager is what uses the itl resources to adjust to international systems.

Normally, you will only require one set of local conventions and since the same set of conventions can be shared by all the applications running under a particular system, the System file contains a copy of each of the international resources. The Mac OS establishes a search path for open resources which responds to a hierarchy starting with the most recently opened resource. A document may contain a resource fork (Hypercard stacks, for instance) but since most do not, the most recently opened is usually the application, followed by the System file. If you want to ensure that a particular set of conventions is always available to users of your application, regardless of the current System, you should install the international resources into the application's resource fork

Most current applications use the "new" resources (itl0, itl1, etc.) but some of the older ones may explicitly require the INTL resources. The System file also includes the INTLs for reverse compatibility and you should keep in mind that you may need to customize the INTLs also. If you have carefully customized some local conventions only to find that an application requires them to be in the INTL 0 resource (or vice versa), open your new resource with the Open Using Hex Editor under the Resource menu, select all the contents and copy them to the clipboard. Then you can open the other resource type, create a new resource, open it using the hex editor and paste.

What can you use this for?

These resources are mostly used by programmers, but the average user can find many uses for the itl0 and itl1. For instance, a person might be used to working on a foreign Macintosh, and would be more accustomed to a different setup. To avoid confusion, they could reset these parameterd to make the formats more similar to what they are used to.

Another possible use is if a person is practicing a foreign language. With the itl1 resource they can set all the values in a date to match the language they are studying.

If you frequently correspond with another country, you can temporarily set the proper values for the parameters, and then all the numbers in your document can be in a format which the recipients will understand.

Dialog Boxes for
the Non-programmer

by Derrick Schneider

Chapter 11

Many Mac programs have certain common attributes, simply because they are Macintosh applications. Menus and icons are two of these common resources. Two other common types are the dialog boxes and the alert boxes. The best example of a dialog box is the one you get when you instruct an application to open a document. This is known as the "Standard File Open Dialog Box" (see Figure 1). Everyone who has tried to throw an

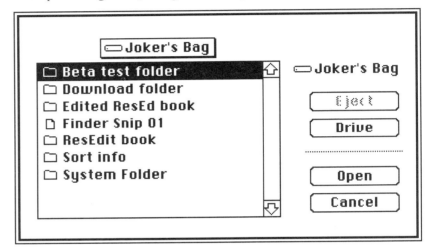

*Figure 1 -
The dialog box one sees
when opening a file*

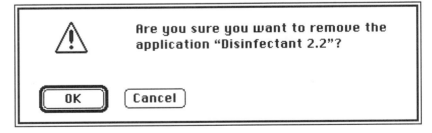

*Figure 2 -
A common alert box*

application into the Trashcan knows what an alert box is (see Figure 2). These are usually accompanied by a beep in order to attract your attention.

Dialog boxes and alert boxes both have certain standard contents. Let's look at each of these items in more depth.

Push buttons are the rounded rectangles within a dialog box which usually contain the words "OK" or "Cancel". They usually dismiss the dialog or alert box. One example of a push button is the "Cancel" button in Figure 1.

Check boxes are usually used by the programmer to indicate an option.

For instance, if the user sees a check box in a dialog, he or she doesn't have to do anything with it; it can just sit there. Thus, it represents an option.

Radio buttons, however, are a little bit different. When a user sees a group of radio buttons, one of them has to be selected (for more about grouping radio buttons, see below). The user does not have the option of leaving them all off. With checkboxes, all of them can be off or on, or any combination between these two extremes. With a group of radio buttons, only one may be selected at a time. Bear in mind that this is only within a group. If there are two or more groups of radio buttons, one in each group must be selected.

Control refers to the scroll bars used in a long list.

Static text is the text which is permanent for the dialog. Looking at Figure 2, the phrase "Are you sure you wish to..." is static text. It cannot be altered in any way within the dialog itself

Editable text is the text which the user types into the dialog box. The most well-known example of this is in the "Save" dialog box of every Macintosh application. When you save a document the first time, you are asked to provide a name. The place where you type this name is an editable text field.

Icons are one type of graphic element one can use in a dialog.

The PICT is the other type of graphic element. The major benefit of a PICT rather than an ICON is that a PICT can be bigger than an ICON, which is limited to 32 pixels by 32 pixels.

UserItems are items which the programmer specifies. These are objects not supported separately by the Dialog Manager within the Toolbox. Some examples of userItems include pop-up menus, thermometers (which indicate progress of an action), and userText, which can be used to create different font styles within a dialog box. Since this item is for programmers, I will not discuss it here.

Editing the Dialog

To get a practice dialog, open a copy of the *Finder* with *ResEdit*. Open the DITL resource within the *Finder* and choose Create New Resource...

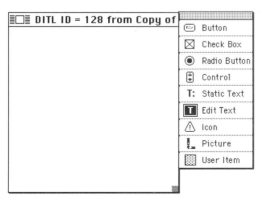

Figure 3 - A blank dialog box and the tool palette

from the Resource menu. *ResEdit* will give you a blank dialog box, with the DITL tool palette, which will look like Figure 3.

To add an item to a dialog box, click and drag the desired tool from the tool palette. You may wish to experiment to see how items with odd sizes (such as really big buttons) are presented within the dialog. For now, create one of each item in your dialog box (except for userItems).

Now we'll talk about acutally editing these items. Right now, your dialog doesn't say much. Your check box has the words "Check Box" next to it, and your radio button has the words "Radio Button" next to it. We want to change these. To edit an item, double-click on it. For instance,

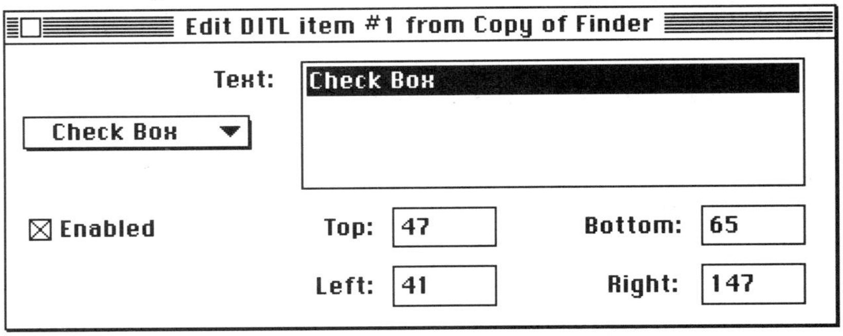

Figure 4 -
The text item editor
for DITLs

double-click on the "Check Box" item. You should get something which looks like Figure 4.

Let's look at each of these parts. There is a pop-up menu on the left, which lets you change in an instant what that item is going to be. For instance, let's say that you had done your dialog box, and realized that you put a check box where you wanted a radio button. Just pull down the pop-up menu, and choose Radio Button. Your item will suddenly be a radio button.

The title of this window indicates that this is DITL item #1. What does this mean? I'll discuss this in more depth later. For now, just realize that each item in a dialog has a number associated with it so that it can be called by the programmer.

The "Text:" box allows you to change the text which appears next to the item, if applicable. This applies to checkboxes, radio buttons, static text, and editable text. In the first three, this text is permanent ; it can't be changed without a copy of ResEdit. In editable text fields, however, this is the default text of the field. For example, when you save an item and are asked what to name the file, most programs will already have a name in this field. You just type over it. This text can be set here.

The "Enabled" checkbox below the pop-up menu allows you to determine whether or not an item is enabled. If this is checked, the user will see a normal checkbox. If this is not checked, the user will see a "greyed-out" item which can not register his or her clicks.

The four fields below the "Text:" field tell you the dimensions of the item. "Top" and "Bottom" indicate what pixel-row the item is in. Similarly, "Left" and "Right" tell you which pixel-column the edges are on. Note that these are relative to the dialog box itself. Thus, in Figure 4, the top edge of the checkbox is 47 pixels from the top of the dialog box. The 0 position is defined as either the topmost row of the dialog or the leftmost edge, depending on the situation.

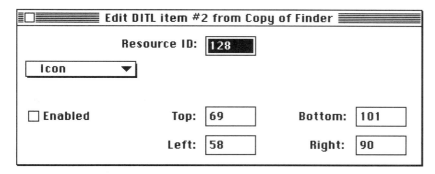

Figure 5 - The graphic item editor for DITLs

Now, these windows can look a little bit different, depending on what item you have selected. In Figure 5, I have opened the item editor for my icon.

This window is almost the same, but it has one important difference. In the checkbox item editor, we had a "Text:" field. In this editor, we can see that the field now says "Resource ID:". This editor allows you to set which icon you wish to use by its ID number. To use a new icon, simply type in its number. If you type in an ID number, and that icon does not exist, ResEdit will show you a generic icon. However, your dialog will not work properly in the program.

Notice the "Enabled" checkbox again. You might be wondering how an icon can be "enabled" or "disabled". Well, programs can be told to look for the user clicking on the icon (or the picture, which has the same editor as this one). Some people might use this to bring up a short piece of info about themselves or the program.

The Menus of the DITL editor

In the **DITL** menu, you can choose a wide variety of commands which help you with your design. Some of these deal with item numbers, which is discussed in more depth below.

Renumber Items... allows you to quickly change the numbering of items. When you choose this menu item, simply hold down the Shift key as you click on the items, in the order that you want them to appear. The first item you click on will always be given the new number 1 (the new numbers show up to the left of the old numbers, which are visible while this command is active), which can lead to trouble if you're not careful. If you want to change the positions of items 4 and 5, your first instinct would be to shift-click on item number 5 and then item number 4. However, this would cause item number 5 to be renumbered to item number 1, and item number 4 to be renumbered to item number 2, and the original item number 1 and item number 2 would then be renumbered. Therefore, you must shift-click on the original item number 1, then item number 2, then item number 3, and then you can rearrange the two items. This way, you keep your original item numbers 1,2, and 3. (You may need to play with this to get a feel for it)

If you select one item by clicking on it once, you can use the menu command **Set Item Number** to give this item a new number. Note, however, that all the other items will be renumbered, so you may wish to do this with caution.

The **Select Item...** command allows you to automatically select an item by its number. Once you type in the number to select, one of your items will become selected, and you can manipulate it.

The **Show Item Numbers** command will, when checked, show all the item numbers of the items in your dialog. The number will appear in the upper right corner of each item. This way, you can quickly see which item is which.

The **Align to Grid** command allows you to set up an invisible grid. This way, the items can only be put on the grid, aligned to one of the lines.

The **Grid Settings...** command allows you to choose the spacing of the grid which your items use.

The **Show All Items** option will force ResEdit to put a rectangle around all the items in the dialog box. This rectangle is the rectangle which is defined in the item editor (pixels from the top, etc.)

The **View As...** command allows you to look at the item in a different font. However, this will not show up in the actual dialog box; it is only for your convenience. Dialog boxes are set at Chicago 12, by default. Except with userItems, this is not changeable as far as I know.

ResEdit 2 is set up so that people can begin publishing software for System 7.0. One of the best proofs of this is the **Balloon Help...** menu command. This allows you to select which "Help ballon resource" you wish to use. If you don't know, System 7.0 will feature the capacity to have help balloons in dialog boxes. Thus, a person who is unsure of what a dialog box item might do will, theroretically, be able to choose a help balloon (if it is made available by the programmer). This might give the user some more insight about what the dialog does.

The **Alignment** menu is fairly self-explanatory; it allows items in a dialog box to be lined up with one another. In order to use this, two or more items must be selected. Select more than one item by holding down the shift key while clicking on each item.

The DLOG and ALRT resources

DITLs only control what appear in a dialog box. Two other resources, DLOG and ALRT, determine whether the dialog box is a regular dialog or an alert.

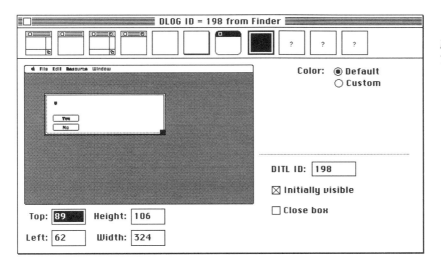

Figure 6 -
The DLOG editor

In Figure 6, I have opened the DLOG editor for a resource in the *Finder*.

The most prominent aspect of the DLOG editor is a miniature version of the Macintosh screen (complete with Desktop pattern). This allows you to position where on the screen your dialog box will appear. To move it, simply hold down the mouse button when on the dialog box, and drag it to its new location. Another important aspect of the DLOG editor is the row of window styles along the top of the screen. Let's look at these one by one. The first from the left is a standard window, complete with scroll bars and a grow box, but missing a zoom box in the upper right corner. The next one is a window with just the close box in the upper left corner. The third is a normal window, with a title bar, close box, zoom box, grow box, and scroll bars. Next is a window with a title bar, close box, and zoom box, but missing everything else. Next is just a plain rectangle. Similar to that is the recatngle with a drop shadow, which can add a little bit of depth to your image. Although it is hard to see due to the fact that it is hilited in my example, the next style is a rectangle with a double border around it. This is a common style for alert boxes. The last three styles can be defined by you, if you have developed a custom Window Definition (WDEF resource), or if you have one you would like to use. At the bottom left corner of the DLOG editor, you can see the measurements (in pixels) of the dialog. As before, 0 is defined as either the top edge of the screen or the the left edge, depending on context. When you have a DLOG, you must tell the Macintosh which DITL resource it is controlling. This is the purpose of the "DITL ID:" field. If you double-click on the sample dialog box on the miniature Macintosh screen, you will bring up the DITL editor for that resource. There are also options for color configuration, as well as determining whether or not a dialog is visible as soon as it is called. The final item is the checkbox for the close box. If this is selected, the window will have a close box. If not, the window won't have a close box in the title bar.

Finally, there is the ALRT resource. This is actually very similar to the DLOG editor, with some slight differences. Again, it allows you to reposition the dialog box and determine its size. It does not have the option of different window styles. Nor does it have the "Initially visible" or "Close box" options. It does still have a field to type in the ID number of the DITL resource you will be using.

In summary, DITLs are the resource which control what items are in a dialog. DLOG and ALRT then determine where the DITL is and what kind of dialog it is: regular or alert.

Numbering

Remember I said earlier that all items in a dialog have a number associated with them? This is very important. If a user clicks on an item, how is that information fed to the program? The answer is: through the numbers. By using the item numbers, a programmmer can tell a program to do one thing if a radio button is "true" (selected) or "false". However, the programmer does not type in: "Tell me what that radio button there says". He or she types in "Get the return from item number 6". The program does not know that it is looking at a radio button; it only tells itself that the result is "true" or "false". Thus, numbering is very important. When a push button is activated, all the items send back info to the program, and it is up to the programmer to work with that. Even items which are not selected send back "false" messages, so that the program knows that that option was not selected.

Items can send back other information as well. Editable text sends back the contents of the field. Static text sends back what it says, but this doesn't change while the dialog box is active.

Certain items have special requirements for numbering. One of these is the default button. When you are presented with a dialog box, you can usually hit <Return> to activate the default button (indicated by a thick, black border). This button is item number 1. It is always a good idea to have item number 1 be a push button. This prevents confusing results. Similarly, item number 2 should be another push button (usually "Cancel"). This can be a little bit different for alerts, but it is not advised.

Another important concept in numbering is with radio buttons. You may have noticed that, when you have a group of radio buttons in a dialog, you can only select one of these. This is due to the numbering of this group of radio buttons. When you assign numbers to them, you must make all the radio buttons in a group sequential and consecutive. In other words, the radio buttons, in order to work properly, must be items 3,4, and 5. They cannot be 3,6, and 8, because then they will all be considered to be separate groups. The Macintosh's Dialog Manager then makes sure that one at a time is selected. If you have two groups, they must be separated by at least one other dialog item.

Other Stuff

As you are going through dialog boxes, looking at the various designs, you may notice some which contain characters such as "^0" or "^1" or something similar. These are place holders for the programmer. When the programmer writes the command which calls up the dialog box, he or she can change the place holders into static text. While the static text will not change within one dialog box, it can be modified each time the dialog is brought up. Again, look at Figure 2, the alert box which appears when you try to throw away an application. If you look at this alert box with ResEdit, you will see a place holder. This way, the programmer can get the name of the application you're tossing out, and then stick it into that place holder.

Most of the time, these place holders get information from the STR# resource within a program. The STR# resource, however, is capable of much more. For instance, open the STR# resource #128 in the Finder (Figure 6)

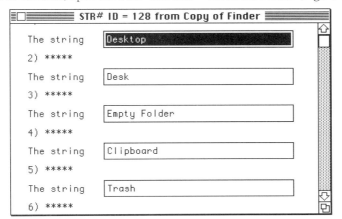

Figure 7 -
The STR# editor

If you look at some of these names, they will no doubt ring a bell. For instance, the word "Trash" at the bottom of my picture. This is the string which the Finder puts under the trashcan. Thus, if you make your trashcan into something different, you may wish to change this string so that it is still relevant to your new icon (*For more information about editing icons, see the icon section at the the beginning of this book*). Also, you will see that, in my picture, the word "Desktop" is highlited. With this, you can change the name of the Desktop file. THIS IS NOT ADVISED AS IT CAN LEAD TO SEVERE ERRORS. NEVER MODIFY THE DESKTOP FILE UNLESS YOU ARE REBUILDING IT. The word "Untitled" is the default name of a newly initialized disk. If you always name your new disks "Blank", you can cange that to the default with this resource. The word "Empty Folder" is the default name of a newly made folder. This can be easily changed to be "New Folder" or something similar. To make any changes to a STR# resource, simply edit the text like you would in any word processor.

Most people who create dialogs are programmers. However, there is nothing to stop you from editing existing dialogs. Some people alter dialog boxes so that the contents say something different. Others like to put in new items which have no meaning at all as practical jokes. However, you should always be careful about editing dialogs. Never change an existing item into another type. The program will probably get very confused if you change a radio button into a checkbox. With this tip in mind, you should be fairly safe.

Customizing Your ImageWriter

by Leonard Morgenstern

Chapter 12

Are you irritated by the ImageWriter's printer driver and its five paper sizes, four of which you never use? Would you rather print 3x5 inch cards, or 9.5 x 6 inch notebook pages? Some word processors make it easy to print these odd sizes: for example, *Microsoft Word* has its Style Sheets. But if your communications program or spreadsheet lacks this flexibility, *ResEdit* will provide you with a means to modify the PREC resources.

```
ImageWriter                                              v2.7      [ OK ]
Quality:        ○ Best        ● Faster      ○ Draft
Page Range:     ● All         ○ From: [    ] To: [    ]   [ Cancel ]
Copies:         [ 1 ]
Paper Feed:     ● Automatic   ○ Hand Feed
Section Range: From: 1        To: 1         ☐ Print Selection Only
☐ Print Hidden Text   ☐ Print Next File
```

First steps

Make a copy of your ImageWriter printer driver (in the System Folder). Move this to another disk or to another folder on your system disk. This will be the copy you work on. Use ResEdit to open this copy, and then open the PREC resource. You are interested in PREC ID number three. Double-click on this, and you should see the PREC editor, shown in Figure 1

Figure 1 - The PREC editor - top

```
▤☐▤▤▤▤▤  PREC ID = 3 from ImageWriter  ▤▤▤
        Number of      [5          ]
        Btns
        Btn 1 Height   [1320]
        Btn 1 Width    [1020]
        Btn 2 Height   [1400]
        Btn 2 Width    [990 ]
        Btn 3 Height   [1680]
        Btn 3 Width    [1020]
        Btn 4 Height   [1440]
        Btn 4 Width    [990 ]
```

The PREC editor

This editor is just a standard *ResEdit* list, such as we saw in the LAYO resource and the FOND resource. To edit a value, simply type over it, just as if you were in a word processor.

The first field in the editor, "Number of Buttons" determines how many different page sizes will be given radio buttons in the printer dialog. The default is five.

The next several fields are labeled, alternately, "Btn x height" and "Btn x width." X represents any number between one and the number of radio buttons you have designated plus one. This is why these fields go from one to six, despite the fact that you only have five buttons. These fields control the heights and widths of the paper size. These are the juicy parts.

The numbers in each of these fields are given in 1/120 of an inch. To determine what size a piece of paper is, divide the values by 120. In the second field, then, we see that the height for "Btn 1" is 1320. If we divide this by 120, we get 11 inches. The width for "Btn 1" can be calculated the same way to yield 8.5 inches. We can now assume that button one represents a standard sheet of paper. Thus, when you add your own values, you have to first multiply the inch measurement by 120 to give you the proper value for the PREC resource.

If you scroll to the end of the PREC editor, you will see a set of fields labeled "Btn x Name" where X again represents any number between one and the number of buttons you have plus one. By looking at them, we can see that these are the names of the buttons in the printer dialogs. In the field "Btn 1 Name," we see that the name of this button is "US Letter." We now know that our earlier assumption was correct. The "Btn 6 Name" field does not have a name, but it does have a '¿' character. This character represents a placeholder. Since this field has to be filled, the programmer put a nonsense

Note that there is no extra space given for the perforated edges of the computer paper. These are assumed to be the standard width, and you do not need to take them into account when changing the size.

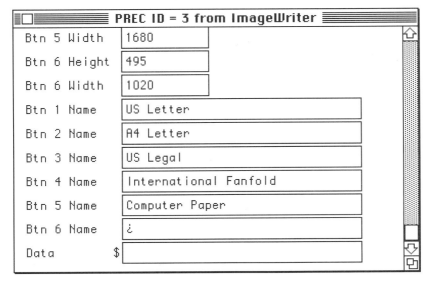

PREC ID = 3 from ImageWriter	
Btn 5 Width	1680
Btn 6 Height	495
Btn 6 Width	1020
Btn 1 Name	US Letter
Btn 2 Name	A4 Letter
Btn 3 Name	US Legal
Btn 4 Name	International Fanfold
Btn 5 Name	Computer Paper
Btn 6 Name	¿
Data	$

*Figure 2 -
The PREC editor -
bottom*

character into it. However, a program can use button six for a custom size by replacing this character.

The final field, "Data", should not be tampered with.

PREC 4 Resources

Some programs have built-in printer drivers, which are designated PREC 4. You modify them the same way as you do PREC 3. They can be found in the PREC resource within an individual application.

Uses for the PREC resource

As mentioned earlier, the only reason for modifying the PREC resource would be to create custom paper sizes on the ImageWriter. Many people no longer use "real" computer paper (the really wide stuff with green and white bands), partly because the ImageWriter II cannot support paper this wide. However, many people might wish to print out their Rolodex cards on the computer, or a set of mailing labels. By altering the measurements of the button, you can set this up fairly quickly.

vers: The Biography of a Program

by Brian Novack

There are aspects of the Macintosh user interface that are always present from the moment your computer has finished its startup process until you shut the machine off. These include things like icons, the menu bar, and the trash can, to name a few. Usually, these features are enough to provide you the information you need to use your favorite word processor, paint program, or communications program without any difficulty. However, there comes a time when each of us needs just a little bit more information than these features allow. This is when we reach for the good old Get Info menu item in the *Finder's* File menu.

With this command, we can discover who wrote the software (so we can call them and beg for free upgrades), when it was written (so we know when it is time to call them for free upgrades), and which version of the software you have (so you don't beg for a free upgrade when you already have the current version and come away looking like a greedy individual.)

```
┌─────────────────────────────────────┐
│ ▤□▤▤▤▤▤ Info ▤▤▤▤▤▤▤▤ │
│                            Locked □  │
│                                      │
│     HyperCard 1.2.5                  │
│                                      │
│   Kind: application                  │
│   Size: 393,103 bytes used, 384K on disk │
│                                      │
│  Where: DPI 44R, DPI SCSI Drive 5    │
│                                      │
│                                      │
│  Created: Mon, Aug 28, 1989, 7:13 AM │
│ Modified: Wed, Sep 20, 1989, 3:33 PM │
│  Version: 1.2.5 Copyright Apple Computer, │
│           Inc. 1987-89               │
│  ┌────────────────────────────────┐  │
│  │                                │  │
│  │                                │  │
│  │                                │  │
│  └────────────────────────────────┘  │
│  Suggested Memory Size (K): 1000     │
│  Application Memory Size (K): │1000│  │
└─────────────────────────────────────┘
```

The Get Info box has two parts:

1)   version information about the software which is the area of our current concern, and

2)   a comment box

The comment box allows the user to type in a comment about the program or file. This information is then stored in an invisible file known as the *Desktop* (one of those special files that we don't play with). This is why rebuilding the *DeskTop* causes this information to be lost. The information in the information section comes from the vers resource.

Using the vers editor

Figure 3-
The vers editor

vers ID = 1 from HyperCard 1.2.5

Version number: 1 . 2 . 5

Release: Final ▼   **Non-release:** 0

Country Code: 00 – USA ▼

Short version string: 1.2.5

Long version string (visible in Get Info):

1.2.5 Copyright Apple Computer, Inc. 1987-89

The vers editor has six areas of information. The version number tells you what the version number is for this application (also seen in the Get Info... dialog box). The Release menu tells you what stage the product is in (see below). If the product is not actually released, there will be information in the non-release area which, together with the Release stage, will tell you how far along the non-release is. There is also a pop-up menu with all of the country codes in the Macintosh System. This tells the Macintosh which international system should be used. The Short Version String will only contain the version number of the application. The Long Version String contains a more detailed description of the version information. All of these areas can be changed rapidly, either by typing in a new value, or by choosing a new option from the pop-up menu.

Zen and the Art of
Resource Editing

Apple has set forth specific guidelines on how to properly number the version information (Apple's Version Numbering Scheme). The first number is the release number (in our example...a 1). Which can be any integer.

This is followed by a period. Following this, is a revision number (a 2 in our example). This represents the revision to the current release number.Finally, the third number (the 5 in our example) is the bug fix to the revision.

Therefore, this is (going backwards) the fifth bug fix, to the second revision, of the first release version of the file.

Release Stages

The vers editor can tell you (or set) the release information about a product. Release stages are the phases that a product goes throught in its trip to a store shelf. Below, the different release stages are explained in more detail.

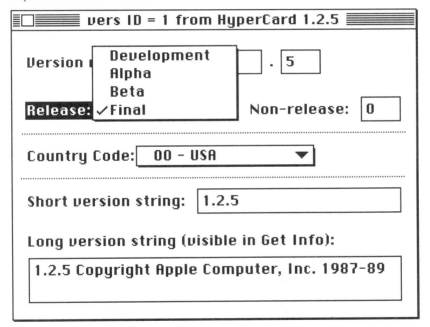

1)   Development: Refers to the very first version of the software created. This is the stage where the programmers are thinking of the initial concepts, features, capabilities. This is also where the interface is usually created.

2)   Alpha: The product features having been defined in the development version, are now being tested to make sure that everything works Macintosh style.

2.0b1
6.0.5
7.0...

Chapter 13
Versions

3)   ßeta: This is where the product is supposed to be stable, and is undergoing final testing to eliminate as many bugs as possible — while still holding to the deadlines set by the Marketing Division of the company producing the software. This may be followed by a number, which indicates which beta release it is. Companies often do more than one. Note, however, the key phrase "supposed to be"

Finally…

5)   Final: Otherwise known as the Release version. This version is supposed to be complete in every respect. Not only will it do everything it's supposed to, but it will fail exactly as it should when asked to do something the developers didn't anticipate you doing.

The non-release stage is used when a programmer makes more than one of the five release stages. For instance, there might be five beta releases before the product is actually released, and they would be numberd (beta 1, beta 2, etc. The non-release stage provides this information

Country Code

This gives your Mac the information it needs to know which country's system you are using. It makes it simple for developers to specify the language to be used by an application.

Currently, this does absolutely nothing… it might do something with System 7.0 — like let you know what country the application was written in, but it won't help you with translating the menus into English from Kanji.

As of the writing of this article, System 6.0.x only uses the *Long version string* information. Future systems are likely to take advantage of the rest of this information, so Apple has decided it's in their best interest to keep this information around.

What can you use this for?

At first, it might seem as if this resource is only good for programmers who are assigning version numbers to their programs. However, there are many good uses of this resource for the average person. For instance, you could modify the vers resource of an application to reflect any modifications you might have made to the application itself. For instance, your *Finder* could say (in the Long Version String) something like "Extra modifications made by…" in its Get Info… dialog. Another useful idea is to use the "Long Version String" to become a permanent comment box which isn't erased when rebuilding the *DeskTop*. Simply type what you want to say into this area of the editor and save your changes.

A Quick Review of the Paint Tools.

by Derrick Schneider

Former versions of ResEdit have had very limited bitmap editors. In the icon windows, for instance, one had two choices of tools: the pencil and the marquee. The pencil was the pointer and would make a black pixel white and a white pixel black. The marquee was available when holding down the Shift key. With this, you could move small parts of the icon, or copy/cut certain parts.

ResEdit 2.1, however, features much more advanced editors. Now all the bitmap resources have a wider variety of tools to choose from.

These tools will be very familiar to those who use paint programs frequently, but a quick review might be handy for those who don't use these applications as often.

The ability to cut, copy and paste objects from one application to another is one of the Mac's greatest features. Recall, however, that something needs to be selected before it can be cut or copied. This is the function of both the lasso tool and the selection rectangle tool. The selection rectangle draws out a rectangular area to be cut or copied. Anything within (or even directly under) the borders of this rectangle will be cut or copied. To use it, click and drag the mouse. This will draw out the rectangle. You can then choose Cut or Copy from the Edit menu. Sometimes, however, one finds that the selection rectangle tool is too limited Perhaps you want to select an area, but a rectangle would select stuff you don't want. This is where the lasso comes in to the picture. Rather than drawing a rectangle, the lasso allows you to define the area which will be selected. Again, click and drag, but this time use the drag to draw out the area you want to select. (This may be a little bit difficult for people like myself, whose freehand abilities are sorely lacking, but a little practice will make it much easier.) Now this area is ready to get put on the clipboard. As a useful short cut, double-clicking on the selection rectangle in the tool area will select the whole editing panel.

The next tool is the pencil tool. This is used to turn "off" or "on" individual pixels (a pixel is "on" if it is black, and "off" if it is white). The bitmap editors of ResEdit show you much enlarged pixels for easy editing, so the pencil tool will turn these large squares off and on. Click on a white pixel to make it black, and vice versa (the pencil tool is slightly different with color editors, but that will be covered in those sections). In older versions of ResEdit, this was the only tool which you had to edit the icons. Thankfully, this is no longer the case!

One of the new tools is the paint bucket. In most of the editors, you'll see a pattern palette (usually a pop-up menu). You can select these patterns simply by clicking on them. With the paint bucket, you can fill an entire

Bitmap refers to anything which uses physical pixels, rather than coding.

For more info about hot spots, see the section about cursors

area with the pattern which you have selected. The "hot spot" (active part) of the cursor is the very tip of the spilling paint. Therefore, to fill a small area, make sure the hot spot is in this area. If you accidentally fill an area (a common enough mistake), you can fix this by immediately choosing **Undo** from the **Edit** menu. If you've clicked somewhere else after making this mistake, however, you cannot undo.

This brings us to the next tool, the eraser. The eraser, as its name implies, will "erase" pixels. It does this by turning off any pixel underneath it when the mouse button is down. It will always make the pixels white, even in the color editors. Use it by clicking and dragging it around inside the editor. In tight corners, you should be careful about using this tool . For areas like this, you can use the pencil to turn off these pixels. ResEdit's eraser is slightly improved from the normal eraser. With most paint programs, you can's see what's under the eraser. In ResEdit, however, the eraser rectangle is transparent. Like the selection rectangle, double-clicking on the eraser tool will erase the whole editing area.

Another useful tool is the line tool. With this tool, you can make straight lines quickly and easily. However, this may not produce the effect which you desire. When the line tool makes "straight" lines, it actually approximates a line. If the line you wish to make is 45°, 90°, or 180°, it will be a straight line. However, any other angle will produce a line which looks jagged. Despite the way it looks, it is nonetheless the straightest line which can be drawn on the computer screen.

The final tools are the shape tools. There are six of these below the other tools: three shaded and three empty. Each of these tools will draw out the shape it looks like (rectangle, rectangle with rounded corners, and ovals). The shaded tools, however, will draw out the shape and fill it with whatever pattern is selected. The hollow tools will just draw the shape, and you will be able to see the pixels "underneath".

Disk Info

This book comes with an 800K floppy disk which contains a variety of programs and artwork which you can use on your own computers. If you did not get a disk with the book, contact the BMUG business office at (415) 549-2684, or leave a message on one of the major information services around the country.

Make a backup copy of this disk, and then lock the master disk. That way, you can work on the backup copy, and not do any permanent damage. The following pages will give you a brief idea of what the contents of this disk are.

1) ResEdit 2.1: This is a self-extracting Compactor™ document. Before you open it, put it onto an empty disk or onto your hard drive. Otherwise, there will not be enough room for the file to decompress. After you have copied it to another place, double-click on the file. This will cause the file to decompress and become useable. ResEdit 2.1™ is a freeware utility provided by Apple Programmers' and Developers' Association (APDA), but Apple retains all copyrights, and you should contact them for information about distributing this program.

2) Keyboard Switcher: This is a cdev written by James Walker, from the University of South Carolina. To use this, place it into your System Folder and restart the computer. Once you have done this, Keyboard Switcher may be configured to your tastes. This program will allow you to set the active KCHR resource and the startup KCHR resource. In addition, Keyboard Switcher will put the corresponding SICN of the KCHR resource in the menubar (Note: System 6.0 or greater is required for this), at the position of your choice. Clicking on this icon will cause a new KCHR to be used. By option-clicking on this icon, you will get a pop-up menu of all the KCHRs available to the System. By command-clicking, you can switch to a different international script setup. Please see the enclosed Read Me! file for information about contacting the author about distributing the program.

3) Façade: This is an INIT written by Greg Marriott, and it allows you to associate icons with various types of disks (hard drive, floppy, etc.). To install it, place it and the file FaçadeIcons into your System Folder and restart the computer. To use it, launch ResEdit and use it to open the FaçadeIcons file. You may paste in your own icons, or use the ones which are provided with the program. Then, use the **Get Resource Info...** dialog box in ResEdit to set the name of the icon to be the same as the disk you wish to associate with that icon. Restart the computer, and your hard drive or floppy will be the icon which you have chosen. For distribution information, contact Mr. Marriott at JusSomeGuy on America Online, or GREG on AppleLink.

4) Sundesk: This INIT allows you to associate icl8s and icl4s with icons which are on your desktop. To install the program, place it in the System Folder and restart the computer. To use the program, open the file with ResEdit and edit the icl8s and icl4s to your taste. Make sure that they have the same ID number as the black and white icon from the Desktop, which you should also paste into the file. The author of this program is Tom Poston, and he should be contacted about distribution information (TPoston on America Online). For a more detailed description, please read the documentation enclosed with the file.

5) Cursor Animator 1.2: This Control Panel device allows you to quickly replace the watch cursor without going through the tedious business of using *ResEdit*. To install a cursor, use the "Load…" button to bring up the standard file dialog box. Then navigate your way to the ResEdit file you wish to use. In Cursor Animator, you will be able to see the name of the cursor (supllied by the name of the acur resource). You can preview these cursors, or rename them. Cursor Animator allows you to have animated cursors for your arrow, I-beam, cross, and plus in addition to your watch. Several public domain cursors have been provided for you to use.

6) KCHR resources is a ResEdit file constructed by Jim Walker. It accompanies his article about the KCHR resource found elsewhere in this book. He has provided several sample keyboard layouts which you may use or edit for practice. These are the KCHR resources in the file. Also included in this file are the SICNs which are associated with the keyboard layouts, and which appear in the menubar when using Keyboard Switcher. Finally, an FKEY named "switchKCHR" is included which you can paste into your System file. This FKEY will toggle between KCHRs installed in your System file. Note: This will not make the active KCHR the startup KCHR, as Keyboard Switcher will do. To activate the FKEY, hit command-shift-7. Any of these resources may be pasted into your System file

The next files are samplings of icon artwork donated to the disk by the authors. These icons are intended to be freely distributable and usable. Our thanks go to the following people for contributing their creative abilities to the disk.

1) Lisa Lee's Color Icons: These icons were donated by Lisa Lee, who wrote the article about icl8s, icl4s, and the ics icons. They include some cartoon characters, an icon of Elvis, and the BMUG mouse.

2) Brian Valente's icons: These icons were contributed by Brian Valente. He has tried to include "artsy" icons as well as practical icons which you can use in *HyperCard* stacks or other programs. He hopes that you will enjoy them

3) DreadEdit: This black and white icon was created by Mikel Evins. If you ever get tired of the standard ResEdit icon, this one should keep you entertained for a while!

Index

Notes

Notes

Notes

Notes

Notes

Notes

Notes

Zen and the Art of
Resource Editing

Notes

Notes

Notes

/